What The  Bible Says About

BIBLICAL SEPARATION

An Examination of 1,896 Bible Verses

By Pastor D. A. Waite, Th.D., Ph.D.
Bible For Today Director

the
**BIBLE
FOR
TODAY**
900 Park Avenue
Collingswood, NJ 08108
Phone: 856-854-4452
www.BibleForToday.org

B.F.T. #4087

What The Bible Teaches About
BIBLICAL SEPARATION

An Examination of 1,896 Bible Verses
By Pastor D. A. Waite, Th.D., Ph.D.
Bible For Today Director

the
**BIBLE
FOR
TODAY**
900 Park Avenue
Collingswood, NJ 08108
Phone: 856-854-4452
www.BibleForToday.org

B.F.T. #4087

Acknowledgments

I wish to acknowledge the assistance of the following people:

- **Yvonne Sanborn Waite**--my wife, for encouraging me to publish this book on Biblical Separation, and for giving other helpful suggestions for the body of the book.
- **Anne Marie Noyle**--a faithful supporter of our **Bible For Today** ministries and an attender via the Internet of our **Bible For Today Baptist Church**, who read the book several times and gave many valuable suggestions.

Published by
THE BIBLE FOR TODAY PRESS
900 Park Avenue
Collingswood, New Jersey 08108
U.S.A.
Pastor D. A. Waite, Th.D., Ph.D.
𝕭𝖎𝖇𝖑𝖊 𝕱𝖔𝖗 𝕿𝖔𝖉𝖆𝖞 𝕭𝖆𝖕𝖙𝖎𝖘𝖙 𝕮𝖍𝖚𝖗𝖈𝖍
Church Phone: 856-854-4747
BFT Phone: 856-854-4452
Orders: 1-800-John 10:9
e-mail: BFT@BibleForToday.org
Website: www.BibleForToday.org
Fax: 856-854-2464
We Use and Defend
The King James Bible
February, 2014
BFT 4087
Copyright, 1954, 1971, 1997, 2014
All Rights Reserved
ISBN #978-1-56848-992-6

Cover Design and Publishing facilitated by:
The Old Paths Publications, Inc.
www.theoldpathspublications.com
706-865-0153

FOREWORD

- **The Reason For This Book.** We are living today when, after almost two thousand years since the New Testament was completed, many genuine born-again Christians seem to have no idea what *Biblical Separation* is all about. Because of this, this subject should be studied and explained clearly for everyone who wishes to read about it.
- **The Background of This Book.** The first draft of *Biblical Separation* was written in 1954 while the author was a graduate student at Dallas Theological Seminary in Texas. The book was revised in both 1971 and 1997. Finally, in 2014, the book has been published for a possible wider readership.
- **The Method Used in This Book.** The author went through the Bible from Genesis through Revelation several times. He wanted to find out what the Bible teaches on the subject of *Bible Separation*. He noted every Bible verse in the Old and New Testaments that dealt with this theme whether directly or by illustration. He found 1,896 verses in all.
- **The Organization of This Book.** In these 132 pages, this important topic of *Biblical Separation* has been divided into six chapters: (1) Preliminary Considerations (2) Separation Regarding Things; (3) Separation Regarding Marriage; (4) Separation Regarding Unbelievers; (5) Separation Regarding Disorderly Believers; and (6) Summary And Conclusions. These chapters are followed by 9 pages of Scripture passages and index of subjects. May the Lord use this book for His glory to wake up genuinely saved Christians to follow God's standards regarding *Biblical Separation*.

D. A. Waite

Pastor D. A. Waite, Th.D., Ph.D.
Director of the **Bible For Today**, Incorporated, and
Pastor of the 𝔅𝔦𝔟𝔩𝔢 𝔉𝔬𝔯 𝔗𝔬𝔡𝔞𝔶 𝔅𝔞𝔭𝔱𝔦𝔰𝔱 𝔈𝔥𝔲𝔯𝔠𝔥

TABLE OF CONTENTS

CHAPTER I
PRELIMINARY CONSIDERATIONS 1

I. THE PROBLEM 1
   A.   The Statement Of The Problem 1
      1.   Questions To Be Answered 1
      2.   The Thesis Stated 1
      3.   Separation Defined What is the definition of
          SEPARATION? 1
          a.   Positive Separation 2
          b.   Negative Separation 2
          c.   Summary 2
      4.   The Bible Our Only Authority On The Doctrine
          Of SEPARATION 2
   B.   The Limitation Of The Problem 2
      1.   Biblical Rather Than Theological 2
      2.   Biblical Rather Than Contemporaneous 2
      3.   Biblical Induction To Be Relied Upon 3
   C.   The Justification Of The Problem 3
      1.   Questions To Be Answered 3
      2.   The Relation Of The N.A.E. and the A.C.C.C. 3
          a.   The A.C.C.C. Position On The N.C.C. 3
          b.   The N.A.E. Position On The N.C.C. 4
II. METHOD OF PROCEDURE 4
   A.   The Statement Of The Method. 4
   B.   The Specific Method Used In This Paper 4
      1.   Four Main Headings Were Found 4
      2.   Scriptures Were Then Arranged Logically Under Each Of
          The Four Headings 5
III. ORGANIZATION OF THE REMAINDER OF THE PAPER ... 5
   A.   The Statement Of Organization 5
      1.   Summary Of Chapter Organization 5
      2.   Chapter Two: SEPARATION REGARDING THINGS ... 5
      3.   Chapter Three: SEPARATION REGARDING
          MARRIAGE 5
      4.   Chapter Four: SEPARATION REGARDING
          UNBELIEVERS 5
      5.   Chapter Five: SEPARATION REGARDING
          DISORDERLY BELIEVERS 6

6. Chapter Six: SUMMARY AND CONCLUSIONS 6
B. Justification Of Organization 6

CHAPTER II
SEPARATION REGARDING THINGS 7

I. SEPARATION REGARDING CANAANITE WAYS AND GOD'S WAYS 7
   A. Separation From Canaanite Ways 7
      1. The Reason For Separation 7
         a. Appreciation For God's Grace To Israel 7
         b. God Wanted Their Bodies To Be Used For Him 7
         c. God Wanted To Keep Pure The Messianic Lineage .. 7
      2. The Command For Separation From Canaanite Ways 8
         a. Leviticus 18:3, 24, 30. 8
         b. Deuteronomy 12:30; 20:17-18. 8
         c. Other Scriptures. 8
           (1) 1 Kings 14:24. 8
           (2) 2 Kings 21:9 and 2 Chronicles 33:2, 9 8
           (3) Ezra 6:21 9
           (4) Ezra 9:1. 9
           (5) Ezekiel 11:12. 9
   B. Separation Unto God's Ways 9
      1. The Reason For Separation Unto God's Ways 9
         a. To Keep From Falling Into Sin 9
         b. To Bring Their State Up To Their Standing 9
      2. The Command For Separation Unto God's Ways 9
         a. Some Of The Scriptures Listed 9
         b. Leviticus 18:4-5, 26. 9
         c. Deuteronomy 4:2, 9. 10
         d. Joshua 1:8. 10
         e. 2 Samuel 22:23. 10
         f. 2 Kings 23:3 10
         g. 1 Chronicles 28:8. 10
II. SEPARATION REGARDING JEWISH CUSTOMS 11
   A. Separation Regarding Days 11
      1. Sabbath Days 11
      2. Feast Days. 11
      3. The Day Of Jubilee. 11
   B. Separation Regarding Diet 11
      1. General Restrictions 11
      2. Eating The Blood Forbidden 11

    3. Special Cases Regarding separation In Diet 12
        a. 1 Kings 13. 12
        b. Daniel 1:8 12
        c. Romans 14:21 And 1 Corinthians 8:13 12
  C, Separation Regarding Property 12
    1. Property Separated Unto The Lord 12
    2. Separation Of Land To The Tribes 12
    3. Levitical Cities And Cities Of Refuge 12
  D. Separation Regarding Disease And Sanitation 12
    1. Separation Regarding Leprosy 13
    2. Separation Regarding Issues 13
    3. Separation Regarding Corpses 13
  E. Separation Regarding Miscellaneous Customs 13
    1. Separation Regarding Mixed Animals 13
    2. Separation Regarding Mixed Seed 13
    3. Separation Regarding Mixed Garments 13
III. SEPARATION REGARDING MONEY AND VALUABLES 14
  A. Valuables Refused 14
    1. Valuables Refused By Abram. 14
    2. Valuables Refused By Elisha 14
    3. Valuables Refused By Peter 14
    1. Money To Build The Tabernacle Separated For Special
       Use 14
    2. Firstfruits Separated For Special Use 15
    3. Tithes Separated For Special Use. 15
    4. Valuables Presented To The Lord For Special Use 15
  C. Valuables Misused 15
    1. Multiplication of Gold And Silver. 15
    2. Multiplication Of Horses 15
    3. Special Cases Of Misuse Of Valuables 15
        a. 1 Kings 15:18. 16
        b. 1 Kings 20:7 16
        c. 2 Kings 5:21-27 16
        d. 2 Kings 16:8. 16
        e. 2 Kings 20:13. 16
        f. 2 Kings 11:1-16 16
IV. SEPARATION REGARDING PLACES. 16
  A. Separation Regarding Places To Leave. 16
    1. Separation in Leaving Ur 16
    2. Separation in Leaving Sodom 16
    3. Separation In Leaving Egypt 17

B. Separation Regarding Places To Avoid 17
      1. Separation In Avoiding Egypt 17
      2. Separation In Avoiding Sinai 17
      3. Separation In Avoiding The Tabernacle 18
         a. The Tabernacle In General 18
         b. Uzziah's Violation Of The Tabernacle 18
   C. Separation Regarding Places To Enter 18
      1. Separation Regarding Entering Canaan 18
      2. Separation Regarding Entering Jerusalem 18
V. SEPARATION REGARDING SPECIFIC SINS 18
   A. The Call To Separation From Sins 18
   B. Separation From The Sin Of Drink 19
      1. Warnings To Separate From Drink. 19
         a. Warnings To The Priests To Separate From Drink .. 19
         b. Warnings To The Nazarites To Separate From
            Drink 19
      2. Examples Of Those Who Failed To Separate From
         Drink 19
      3. Examples Of Those Who Separated From Drink 19
   C. Separation From The Sin Of Idolatry. 19
      1. Warnings To Separate From Idolatry 19
      2. Examples Of Those Who Failed To Separate From
         Idolatry 20
         a. Exodus 32 20
         b. Leviticus 17:7 20
         c. Judges 2:12. 20
         d. Other Examples of Israel's Idolatry 20
   D. Separation From The Sin Of Sensuality. 21
      1. Warnings To Separate From Sensuality. 21
         a. Warnings To Separate From Prostitution 21
         b. Warnings To Separate From Homosexuality 21
      2. Examples Of Those Who Failed To Separate From
         Sensuality 21
         a. The People of Judah 21
         b. Lot 21
         c. Judah 21
         d. Other Examples Of Israel's Sensuality 21

CHAPTER III
SEPARATION REGARDING MARRIAGE 23
I. DISPENSATIONAL ASPECTS OF MARRIAGE 23
   A. The Dispensations Defined. 23
      1. The Dispensation Of Innocence 23
      2. The Dispensation of Conscience 23
      3. The Dispensation Of Human Government 23
      4. The Dispensation of Promise 23
      5. The Dispensation Of Law 24
      6. The Dispensation Of Grace 24
      7. The Dispensation Of Kingdom 24
   B. The Dispensations Involved 24
      1. Marriage In The Dispensation Of Innocence 24
      2. Marriage In The Dispensation Of Conscience 24
      3. Marriage In The Dispensation of Promise 24
      4. Marriage In The Dispensation Of Law 25
      5. Marriage In The Dispensation Of Grace 25
   C. The Applicability of Separation In Marriage Teaching 25
      1. Marriage Occurred In Every Dispensation 25
      2. Marriage Is Like Ethics 25
      3. Marriage Principles A Constant 25
II. EXAMPLES OF SEPARATED MARRIAGES 25
   A. The Lessons On Separation In Marriage From Eden 25
      1. The Purpose Of A Wife 26
         a. To Be A Helper 26
         b. To Meet A Need 26
      2. The Nature Of The Wife. 26
         a. Eve Was Taken From The Man. 26
         b. Eve Was A Similar Creature To The Man 26
      3. The Number Of Wives. 26
         a. The Word, "Wife," Is Singular 26
         b. The Expression,"One Flesh," Is Singular 27
   B. Examples Of SEPARATED Marriages 27
      1. Old Testament Examples Of SEPARATED Marriages. . . 27
         a. The SEPARATED Marriage Of The Parents Of Moses 27
         b. The SEPARATED Marriage Of Elimelech And Naomi 27
      2. New Testament Examples Of SEPARATED Marriages . 27

       a. The SEPARATED Marriage Of Zacharias And Elizabeth 27
       b. The SEPARATED Marriage Of Joseph And Mary . 27
       c. The SEPARATED Marriage Of Aquila And Priscilla 28

III. **MARRIAGES WITH THE HEATHEN** 28
  A. Teaching Against Unseparated Marriages With The Heathen .. 28
    1. Teaching Against Unseparated Marriages By The Patriarchs 28
    2. Teaching Against Unseparated Marriages By Pre-Exilic Teaching 28
       a. Moses' Teaching To Israel Against Unseparated Marriages 28
       b. Joshua's Teaching To Israel Against Unseparated Marriages 29
       c. Samson's Parents' Teaching To Samson Against Unseparated Marriages 29
    3. Teaching Against Unseparated Marriages fly Post-Exilic Teaching 29
       a. Ezra's Teaching Against Unseparated Marriages ... 29
       b. Nehemiah's Teaching Against Unseparated Marriages 29
  B. Reasons Against Unseparated Marriages With The Heathen ... 29
    1. Reasons Against Unseparated Marriages That Concern God. 29
       a. So The People Would Not Transgress 29
       b. So The People Would Not Turn Away 30
       c. So the People Would Not Be Idolaters 30
    2. Reasons Against Unseparated Marriages That Concern .. 30
       a. So the Lord Would Drive Out The Canaanites 30
       b. So The Heathen Would Not Be Snares. 30
       c. So Israel Would Be Blessed In The Land 31
       d. So The Israelites Would Speak Purely 31
  C. Instances Of Unseparated Marriages With The Heathen 31
    1. Instances Of Unseparated Marriages In-The Time Of The Patriarchs 31
       a. Esau's Unseparated Marriage With The Heathen ... 31
       b. Judah's Unseparated Marriage With The Heathen .. 31
       c. Joseph's Unseparated Marriage With The Heathen .. 31
    2. Instances Of Unseparated Marriages In The Time Of The Wanderings 32

- a. Moses' Unseparated Marriage With The Heathen .. 32
- b. An Israelitish Woman's Unseparated Marriage With The Heathen 32
- c. Israel's Unseparated Marriages With The Heathen Moabites 32
- 3. Instances Of Unseparated Marriages In The Time Of The Judges 33
  - a. Israel's Unseparated Marriages With The Heathen Canaanites 33
  - b. Gideon's Unseparated Marriage With The Heathen 33
  - c. Samson's Unseparated Marriage With The Heathen 33
  - d. Naomi's Sons' Unseparated Marriages With The Heathen 34
  - e. Boaz's Unseparated Marriage With Ruth The Moabitess 34
- 4. Instances Of Unseparated Marriages In The Time Of The Kings 34
  - a. Solomon's Unseparated Marriages With The Heathen 34
  - b. Ahab's Unseparated Marriage With The Heathen .. 34
  - c. Jorum's Unseparated Marriage With The Heathen .. 35
  - d. Jehoshaphat's Unseparated Marriage With The Heathen 35
  - e. Three Evil Mothers' Unseparated Marriage Ideas .. 35
    - (1) Naamah 35
    - (2) Maachah 35
    - (3} Athaliah 35
- 5. Instances Of Unseparated Marriages in the Time of the Post-Exile 35
  - a. Ezra's People's Unseparated Marriages With The Heathen 35
  - b. Nehemiah's People's Unseparated Marriages With The Heathen 36
  - c. Esther's Unseparated Marriage With The Heathen . 36

IV. **NEW TESTAMENT TEACHING ON SEPARATED MARRIAGE** 36
- A. Apparent Exceptions To Separated Marriage 36
  - 1. 1 Corinthians 7, As An Apparent Exception To Separated Marriage 36
    - a. The Need For Marriage 36
    - b. The Marital Duties Of Husbands And Wives 36

        c. Widows, Bachelors, And Separations 37
        d. The Case Of A Man Having An Unbelieving Wife . 37
        e. The Case Of A Woman Having An Unbelieving
           Husband 37
        f. 1 Corinthians 7 NOT An Exception To
           The SEPARATED Marriage Rule At All 37
    2. 1 Peter 3, As An Apparent Exception To Separated
       Marriage. 37
       a. The Problem 37
       b. Two Possible Explanations 37
         (1) Possibly A Disobedient Christian Is In Mind . . 37
         (2) Possibly A Marriage When Both Were
            Unsaved 37
 B. Scriptures Implying Separated Marriage 38
   1. 1 Timothy 3:11 Implies SEPARATED Marriage 38
   2. 1 Peter 3:7 Implies SEPARATED Marriage 38
   3. 2 Corinthians 6:14-18 Implies SEPARATED Marriage . . 38
 C. Scriptures Demanding Separated Marriage 38
   1. Ephesians 5:22-33 Demands SEPARATED Marriage ... 38
      a. The Background 38
      b. The Verses Could Not Be Fulfilled If An
         Unseparated Marriage Were In View 39
      c. The Analogy Of Christ And The Church 39
      d. This Analogy Could Not Be Used If Not
         A SEPARATED Marriage In View 39
      e. This Analogy Tends To Prove Marriage Principles
         Are Unchangeable 39
   2. Revelation 19:7-9 Demands SEPARATED Marriage 39
      a. The Setting 39
      b. The Church Has Been Raptured 40
      c. The Bride Could Not Be Unsaved and
         UNSEPARATED 40
      d. This Passage Illustrates God's Ideal Of
         SEPARATED Marriage 40

CHAPTER IV
SEPARATION REGARDING UNBELIEVERS 41
I. ISRAEL'S SEPARATION REGARDING THE CANAANITES ... 41
 A. Separation Teaching Regarding The Canaanites 41
   1. The Canaanites Were To Be Removed. 41
      a. The Remover Of The Canaanites 41

  b. The Reason For The Removal Of The Canaanites .. 41
  c. The Method Of Removal Of The Canaanites 41
 2. Israel's Instructions Regarding SEPARATION From
  The Canaanites 42
  a. Separation From Canaanites Regarding Covenants . 42
  b. SEPARATION From Canaanites Regarding
   Fellowship 42
  c. SEPARATION From Canaanites Regarding
   Marriage 42
  d. SEPARATION From Canaanites Regarding
   Idolatry 42
 B. Obedience To The SEPARATION Teaching Regarding
  The Canaanites 43
  1. Obedience To The SEPARATION From Canaanites in
   the Time Of Moses. 43
  a. SEPARATION From Sihon 43
  b. SEPARATION From Og 43
  2. Obedience To The SEPARATION From Canaanites In
   The Time Of Joshua 43
 C. Disobedience To The SEPARATION From Canaanites 43
  1. Disobedience To SEPARATION Regarding Their
   Removal 43
  2. Disobedience To SEPARATION Regarding Covenants . 44
  3. Disobedience To SEPARATION From Canaanites
   Regarding Fellowship 44
  4. Disobedience to SEPARATION Regarding Marriage ... 44
II. **FAILURE IN SEPARATION REGARDING
 UNBELIEVERS IN GENERAL** 44
 A. Failure in SEPARATION With Unbelievers In The Time Of
  The Patriarchs 44
  1. Abram's Failure In SEPARATION From Unbelievers ... 44
  2. Lot's Failure In SEPARATION From Unbelievers 45
  a. Lot's Failure In SEPARATION By His Choice Of
   Sodom 45
  b. Lot's Failure In SEPARATION by His Contest With
   The Sodomites 45
  c. Lot's Failure In SEPARATION By His Desire to
   Remain In Sodom 45
  3. Esau's Failure In SEPARATION From Unbelievers 45
  4. Dinah's Failure In SEPARATION From Unbelievers ... 45

5. Joseph's Brethren And Their Failure In SEPARATION From Unbelievers 45
6. Judah's Failure In SEPARATION From Unbelievers ... 46
7. Jacob's Failure In SEPARATION From Unbelievers 46
B. Failure In SEPARATION With Unbelievers In The Time Of Moses And The Judges. 46
  1. Moses' Failure In SEPARATION From Unbelievers 46
  2. Israel's Failure In SEPARATION From The Moabite Unbelievers 46
  3. Samson's Failure In SEPARATION From Unbelievers .. 46
  4. Elimelech And Naomi's Failure In SEPARATION From Unbelievers 46
C. Failure In SEPARATION From Unbelievers In The Time Of The Kings 47
  1. Failure In SEPARATION From Unbelievers In The United Kingdom 47
     a. Saul's Failure In SEPARATION From Unbelievers . 47
     b. David 'a Failure In SEPARATION From Unbelievers 47
        (1) David And The Philistines 47
        (2) David and Hanun 47
     c. Solomon's Failure In SEPARATION From Unbelievers. 47
        (1) Solomon And Pharaoh 47
        (2) Solomon And Hiram 47
        (3) Solomon And The Queen of Sheba 48
        (4) Solomon And Egyptian Horses 48
        (5) Solomon And Wives 48
  2. Failure In SEPARATION From Unbelievers In The Divided Kingdom 48
     a. Abijam's Failure In SEPARATION From Unbelievers 48
     b. Asa's Failure In SEPARATION From Unbelievers . 48
     c. Ahab's Failure In SEPARATION From Unbelievers 48
        (1) Ahab And Jezebel 48
        (2) Ahab And Syria 48
     d. Jehoshaphat's Failure In SEPARATION From Unbelievers 49
        (1) Jehoshaphat And Ahab. 49
        (2) Jehoshaphat And Ahaziah 49

  e. Ahaziah's Failure In SEPARATION From
    Unbelievers 49
  f. Amaziah's Failure In SEPARATION From
    Unbelievers 49
  g. Uzziah's Failure In SEPARATION From
    Unbelievers 49
  h. Ahaz's Failure In SEPARATION from Unbelievers 49
  . Hezekiah's Failure In SEPARATION From
    Unbelievers 50
    (1) Hezekiah And Egypt 50
    (2) Hezekiah and Babylon 50
  j. Josiah's Failure in SEPARATION From
    Unbelievers 50
 D. Failure In SEPARATION From Unbelievers In The Time Of
  The Post-Exile 50
  1. Ezra's People's Failure In SEPARATION From
   Unbelievers 50
  2. Nehemiah's People's Failure In SEPARATION
   From Unbelievers 51
   a. Nehemiah's People's Failure In
    SEPARATION Regarding Marriage 51
   b. Nehemiah's People's Failure In
    SEPARATION Regarding Traders 51
  3. Esther's Failure In SEPARATION From Unbelievers ... 51
III. SUCCESS IN SEPARATION REGARDING UNBELIEVERS .. 51
 A. Success In SEPARATION With Unbelievers In The Time
  Of The Patriarchs 51
  1. Enoch's Success In SEPARATION From Unbelievers ... 51
  2. Noah's Success In SEPARATION From Unbelievers ... 52
  3. Abram's Success in SEPARATION From Unbelievers .. 52
   a. Abram And Sodom 52
   b. Abram And Ephron 52
  4. Jacob's Success In SEPARATION From Unbelievers ... 52
   a. Jacob And Laban 52
   b. Jacob And Burial 52
  5. Joseph's Success In SEPARATION From Unbelievers .. 53
 B. Success In SEPARATION From Unbelievers In The Time Of
  The Kings 53
  1. Asa's Success In SEPARATION From Unbelievers 53
   a. Asa And Ethiopia 53
   b. Asa and Maachah 53

2. Jehoshaphat's Success In SEPARATION From Unbelievers 53
3. Elijah's Success In SEPARATION From Unbelievers ... 53
4. Jehu's Success in SEPARATION From Unbelievers 53
5. Jehoida's Success In SEPARATION From Unbelievers .. 53
6. Hezekiah's Success In SEPARATION From Unbelievers 54
C. Success In SEPARATION From Unbelievers In The Time Of The Exile 54
   1. Daniel's Success in SEPARATION From Unbelievers ... 54
      a. Daniel And Food 54
      b. Daniel and Prayer 54
   2. Shadrach, Meshach, and Abednego's Success In SEPARATION From Unbelievers 54
      a. Regarding Food 54
      b. Regarding Idolatry 54
   3. Jeremiah's Success In SEPARATION From Unbelievers . 54
      a. Jeremiah's Sitting Alone 54
      b. Jeremiah's Staying In The Land 55
D. Success In SEPARATION From Unbelievers In The Time Of The Post-Exile 55
   1. Ezra's Success In SEPARATION From Unbelievers 55
      a. Ezra And His Helpers 55
      b. Ezra And The Soldiers 55
      c. Ezra's People And Marriage 55
   2. Nehemiah's Success In SEPARATION From Unbelievers 55
      a. Nehemiah's People And Strangers 55
      b. Nehemiah And The Mixed Multitude 55
   3. Mordecai's Success In SEPARATION From Unbelievers 55

IV. NEW TESTAMENT SEPARATION REGARDING UNBELIEVERS 56
A. Separation In The New And Old Testaments Compared 56
   1. Old And New Testament SEPARATION Compared Regarding The People Concerned 56
   2. Old And New Testament SEPARATION Compared Regarding The Place. 56
   3. Old And New Testament SEPARATION Compared Regarding God's Purpose 56
B. SEPARATION In The Time Of The Lord Jesus Christ 56

1. SEPARATION In The Time Of The Lord Jesus Christ in Regard to Christ Himself. 56
   a. Christ And Satan 56
   b. Christ And The Syro-Phoenician Woman 56
   c. Christ And Sinners 57
   d. Christ And The Samaritan Woman 57
   e. Christ and The World 57
2. SEPARATION In The Time Of The Lord Jesus Christ In Regard To The Twelve Apostles 57
3. SEPARATION In The Time Of The Lord Jesus Christ In Regard To Peter. 57
4. SEPARATION In The Time Of The Lord Jesus Christ In Regard To The Upper Room Teaching 57
C. SEPARATION In The Time Of The Book Of Acts 57
D. SEPARATION In The Epistles And The Book Of Revelation. 58
   1. SEPARATION In The Epistles Of Paul. 58
      a. SEPARATION In The Book Of Romans 58
      b. SEPARATION In The Books Of 1 And 2 Corinthians 58
         (1) 1 Corinthians 58
         (2) 2 Corinthians 58
      c. SEPARATION in The Book Of Ephesians 58
      d. SEPARATION In The Book Of Philippians 58
   2. SEPARATION In the General Epistles 59
      a. SEPARATION In The Book Of James 59
      b. SEPARATION In The Book Of 1 John 59
      c. SEPARATION In The Book Of 2 John 59
   3. SEPARATION In The Book Of Revelation 59

CHAPTER V
SEPARATION REGARDING DISORDERLY BELIEVERS 61
I. DEFINITION OF TERMS 61
   A. "Believers" Defined 61
   B. "Orderly" Defined 61
   C. "Disorderly" Defined 61
   D. "SEPARATION" Defined 62
II. SEPARATION REGARDING ORDERLY BELIEVERS 62
   A. The SEPARATION Of Orderly Believer, Bezaleel 62
   B. The SEPARATION Of The Nazarites As Orderly Believers .. 62

		1.	The Rules For Nazarites 62
		2.	Samson The Nazarite 63
		3.	Failures of Nazarites 63
	C.	The SEPARATION Of The Levites As Orderly Believers 63
		1.	The Regular Levites 63
			a. The SEPARATION Of The Regular Levites 63
			b. The General Duties Of The Regular Levites 63
			c. The Special Duties Of The Regular Levites 63
		2.	The Priests. 64
			a. The Priestly Family Of Aaron 64
			(1) Korah's Rebellion 64
			(2) Aaron's Family Set Apart 64
			b. The High Priest 64
			(1) Aaron As High Priest 64
			(2) Aaron's Successors 64
	D.	The SEPARATION Of The Prophets As Orderly Believers ... 65
		1.	The Purpose Of The Prophets 65
			a. The Purpose Of The Prophets Expressed 65
			b. The Purpose Of The Prophets Illustrated 65
			(1) Ahijah, Jehu, and Eliab As Prophets 65
			(2) Shemiah, Zechariah, and Obed As Prophets .. 65
			(3) Urijah, Jeremiah, ant Haggai As Prophets 65
			(4) All The Other Prophets 65
		2.	The Reception Of The Prophets 66
			a. The Prophetic Message Unheeded 66
			b. Some Prophets Were Punished 66
			c. Some Prophets Were Killed 66
		3.	The Failures Of The Prophets 66
			a. Failures Of Some Prophets In Their Personal Life .. 66
			(1) They were drunken 66
			(2) They were asleep 66
			(3) They were ashamed 66
			(4) They were covetous 66
			(5) They dealt falsely 66
			(6) They were wicked 66
			(7) They were adulterous 66
			(8) They were liars 66
			(9) They were light 66
			(10) They were out for money 66
			(11) They were fools 66
			(12) They were as bad as Sodom and Gomorrah ... 67

  b. Failures Of Some Prophets In Their Preaching 67
   (1) They taught lies 67
   (2) They prophesied by Baal 67
   (3) They prophesied falsely 67
   (4) They strengthened the hand of evildoers 67
   (5) They were without God's message 67
  c. Failures of Some Prophets In Their Results 67
   (1) They did not cause Israel to hear the Words of God 67
   (3) They caused Israel to err 67

III. **OLD TESTAMENT SEPARATION REGARDING DISORDERLY BELIEVERS** 67
 A. Old Testament SEPARATION Regarding Disorderly Believers By Leaving 67
  1. SEPARATION By The Disorderly Leaving The Orderly 68
   a. Disorderly Cain Leaving Orderly Adam and Eve .. 68
   b. Disorderly Lot Leaving Orderly Abram 68
   c. Disorderly Hagar Leaving Orderly Abram And Sarai 68
   d. Disorderly Lepers Leaving Orderly Israel 68
   e. Disorderly Manslayers Leaving Orderly Israel 68
   f. Disorderly Unclean Persons Leaving Orderly Clean Israelites 68
  2. SEPARATION By The Orderly Leaving The Disorderly 69
   a. Orderly Abram Leaving Disorderly Lot 69
   b. Orderly Jacob Leaving Disorderly Esau 69
   c. Orderly Joseph Leaving Disorderly Brothers 69
   d. Orderly Levites Leaving Disorderly Israelites 69
   e. Orderly Moses and Aaron Leaving Disorderly Israel 69
   f. Orderly Moses And The Judges Of Israel Leaving Disorderly Israelites 69
   g. Orderly David Leaving Disorderly Saul 70
   h. Orderly Israel's Leaving Disorderly Rehoboam 70
 B. Old Testament SEPARATION Regarding Disorderly Believers By Death 70
  1. SEPARATION by The Disorderly Being "Cut Off." 70
   a. SEPARATION Of The Disorderly by Being Cut Off Regarding Circumcision 70
   b. SEPARATION of the Disorderly By Being Cut Off Regarding Leaven 70

- c. SEPARATION Of The Disorderly By Being Cut Off Regarding Incense. 70
- d. SEPARATION of the Disorderly By Being Cut Off Regarding The Sabbath 71
- e. SEPARATION of the Disorderly By Being Cut Off Regarding The Peace Offerings 71
- f. SEPARATION of the Disorderly by Being Cut Off Regarding Fat 71
- g. SEPARATION of the Disorderly By Being Cut Off Regarding Blood 71
- h. SEPARATION of the Disorderly by Being Cut Off Regarding Offerings 71
- I. SEPARATION of the Disorderly By Being Cut Off Regarding Sexual Offences 71
- j. SEPARATION of the Disorderly By Being Cut Off Regarding Molech 71
- k. SEPARATION Of the Disorderly by Being Cut Off Regarding Wizards. 72
- l. SEPARATION of the Disorderly By Being Cut Off Regarding The Day Of Atonement 72
- m. SEPARATION of the Disorderly By Being Cut Off Regarding The Passover 72
- n. SEPARATION of the Disorderly By Being Cut Off Regarding Sinning. 72
- o. SEPARATION of the Disorderly By Being Cut Off Regarding Purification 72
2. SEPARATION By The Disorderly Being Put To Death .. 72
    - a. SEPARATION of the Disorderly By Death Regarding Sinai. 73
    - b. SEPARATION of the Disorderly By Death Regarding Murder 73
    - c. SEPARATION of the Disorderly By Death Regarding Kidnaping 73
    - d. SEPARATION of the Disorderly by Death Regarding 73
    - e. SEPARATION of the Disorderly By Death Regarding Oxen 73
    - f. SEPARATION of the Disorderly by Death Regarding The Sabbath 73
    - g. SEPARATION of the Disorderly By Death Regarding 73

  h. SEPARATION of the Disorderly by Death
    Regarding Wizards 74
  i. SEPARATION of the Disorderly by Death
    Regarding Sexual Offenses 74
  j. SEPARATION of the Disorderly By Death
    Regarding The Tabernacle 74
  k. SEPARATION of the Disorderly by Death
    Regarding False Prophets 74
  l. SEPARATION of the Disorderly By Death
    Regarding Idolatry 74
  m. SEPARATION of the Disorderly By Death
    Regarding Disobedient Sons. 75
  n. SEPARATION of the Disorderly by Death
    Regarding Disobedience To Joshua 75
  o. SEPARATION of the Disorderly by Death
    Regarding Spoil 75
  p. SEPARATION of the Disorderly by Death
    Regarding Belial 75
  q. SEPARATION of the Disorderly by Death
    Regarding Mispah 75
  r. SEPARATION of the Disorderly by Death
    Regarding Shimei 75
  s. SEPARATION of the Disorderly by Death
    Regarding Seeking The Lord 76
  t. SEPARATION of the Disorderly by Death
    Regarding Adonijah. 76
IV. **NEW TESTAMENT SEPARATION REGARDING DISORDERLY BELIEVERS** 76
 A. Definition of Terms. 76
  1. "Believers." 76
  2. "Orderly." 76
  3. Disorderly." 76
  4. "SEPARATION." 77
 B. Passages On New Testament SEPARATION From Disorderly 77
  1. New Testament SEPARATION Passages From
    Disorderly Believers That Are Disputed. 77
    a. 1 Timothy 6:1-5. 77
    b. 2 Timothy 2:20-21. 77
    c. 2 Timothy 4:14-15 78
    d. Titus 3:8-11. 78

2. New Testament SEPARATION Passages From
Disorderly Believers That Are Clear 79
  a. 1 Corinthians 5:1-13 Clearly Teaches
     SEPARATION From Disorderly Believers. 79
     (1) The Sin Of Incest in 1 Corinthians 5 79
     (2) Paul Denounced The Corinthian Attitude
         Toward This Sin. 79
     (3) The Difficulty of TOTAL Separation Or
         Contact With The World Of Sinners 79
     (4) Paul Taught Clearly TOTAL SEPARATION
         From A disorderly Christian Fornicator or
         Similar Sinner 80
  b. 2 Thessalonians 3:6-15 Clearly Teaches
     SEPARATION From Disorderly Believers 80
     (1) The General Problem Of Christian
         "disorderliness." 80
     (2) Paul's Example Of Orderliness 80
     (3) Paul Taught Clearly TOTAL SEPARATION
         From A Disorderly Christian In This Case 80

CHAPTER VI
SUMMARY AND CONCLUSIONS 83

I. SEPARATION REGARDING THINGS 83
   A. SEPARATION Regarding Canaanite Ways And God's Ways .. 83
      1. Summary 83
      2. Conclusions. 83
   B. SEPARATION Regarding Jewish Customs 83
      1. Summary 83
      2. Conclusions 83
   C. SEPARATION Regarding Money And Valuables. 84
      1. Summary 84
      2. Conclusions 84
   D. SEPARATION Regarding Places 84
      1. Summary 84
      2. Conclusions 84
   E. SEPARATION Regarding Specific Sins 85
      1. Summary 85
      2. Conclusions 85
II. SEPARATION REGARDING MARRIAGE 85
    A. The Dispensational Aspects Of Marriage. 85
       1. Summary. 85

		2. Conclusions 85
	B.	Examples of SEPARATED Marriage 85
		1. Summary..................................... 85
		2. Conclusions 86
	C.	Marriages With Heathen 86
		1. Summary..................................... 86
		2. Conclusions 86
	D.	New Testament Teaching On SEPARATED Marriage 87
		1. Summary..................................... 87
		2. Conclusions 87
III.	SEPARATION REGARDING UNBELIEVERS 87
	A.	Israel's SEPARATION Regarding The Canaanites 87
		1. Summary..................................... 87
		2. Conclusions 87
	B.	Examples of SEPARATION Regarding Unbelievers 88
		1. Summary..................................... 88
		2. Conclusions 88
	C.	Success In SEPARATION Regarding Unbelievers 89
		1. Summary..................................... 89
		2. Conclusions 89
	D.	New Testament SEPARATION Regarding Unbelievers 90
		1. Summary..................................... 90
		2. Conclusions 90
IV.	SEPARATION REGARDING DISORDERLY BELIEVERS 90
	A.	Definition of Terms 90
		1. Summary..................................... 90
		2. Conclusions 90
	B.	SEPARATION Regarding Orderly Believers 91
		1. Summary..................................... 91
		2. Conclusions 91
	C.	Old Testament SEPARATION Regarding Disorderly Believers. 91
		1, Summary..................................... 91
		2. Conclusions 91
	D.	New Testament SEPARATION Regarding Disorderly Believers. 91
		1. Summary..................................... 91
		2. Conclusions 92
Index Of Words And Phrases 93
About The Author 97
Order Blanks 98

The *Defined King James Bible* Order Blank 105

CHAPTER I
PRELIMINARY CONSIDERATIONS

The Subject of "THE BIBLICAL TEACHING ON SEPARATION" is one of the most important subjects facing the church today. For the Christian believers to be in ignorance of what the Bible has to teach concerning this vast subject of SEPARATION is to insure the victory of the coming apostasy and to vitiate God's plan and will for His born again, blood-bought children.

In this first chapter, we will discuss (1) The problem, (2) the method of procedure, and (3) the organization of the remainder of the paper. The basic research from the Bible on this subject of "BIBLICAL SEPARATION" was done by the writer in 1954. As it is now being written and published in 1971 (and again in 1997), certain up-dating is being done, but the Biblical verses and teaching remain the same and without change.

I. THE PROBLEM

A. The Statement Of The Problem. The general theme of this paper is the subject of the doctrine of SEPARATION. Throughout the Bible the subject of SEPARATION is discussed by implication and picture, illustration and shadow.

    1. Questions To Be Answered. When the subject is narrowed down to "BIBLICAL TEACHING ON SEPARATION," this field of the doctrine of SEPARATION is narrowed appreciably, making the primary point of the investigation, not theological or practical, so much as BIBLICAL. Some of the questions to be answered in this study will be: (1) Does the Bible teach anything in an authoritative manner on this doctrine? (2) Is there any absolute stand that the Scripture takes with regard to SEPARATION? (3) Has God left Himself without a witness, Biblically speaking, when it comes to this important field of study? The problem of this paper is to answer some of these questions.

    2. The Thesis Stated. It will be the thesis of this project to assume that **THE BIBLE DOES DEFINITELY SPEAK REGARDING THIS DOCTRINE SO AS TO MAKE IT UNNECESSARY FOR THE CHILD OF GOD TO REMAIN IN IGNORANCE AS TO HIS SEPARATED WALK IN THE MIDST OF A CROOKED AND PERVERSE GENERATION AMONG WHOM HE IS SUPPOSED TO SHINE AS A LIGHT IN THE WORLD.** (Philippians 2:15)

    3. Separation Defined What is the definition of SEPARATION? This question is one that must be dealt with at the outset in a brief fashion only, since it will be elaborated on by the later chapters of the paper. SEPARATION, as it is used in this paper, is defined both positively and negatively.

        a.   **Positive Separation.** In a positive fashion, it is to be the believer's complete YIELDEDNESS UNTO HIS GOD AND FATHER TO DO AS HE ALONE DIRECTS IN EVERY AVENUE OF HIS LIFE.

        b.   **Negative Separation.** Negatively considered it is THE ATTITUDE OF THE BELIEVER TOWARD SIN AND THINGS CONNECTED WITH IT THAT WOULD MAKE HIM WITHDRAW FROM ANYTHING THAT IS SO DEGRADED AND MADE LOW THAT IT IS UNBEFITTING TO HIS WALK BEFORE GOD TO INDULGE HIMSELF IN IT.

        c.   **Summary.** Briefly stated, then, SEPARATION **unto God** is the positive aspect while SEPARATION **from sin** is the negative aspect of this Biblical doctrine.

    4.   **The Bible Our Only Authority On The Doctrine Of SEPARATION.** As the Biblical passages are brought up for discussion and exposition, it will become evident that God has called the believer to both a positive and a negative type of SEPARATION as he is walking here below in a world of sin and sinners. Since the Bible has been left for us to read and meditate on and since it is our EXCLUSIVE AUTHORITY in ALL matters of life, having been verbally and plenarily inspired and infallibly and inerrantly written, it is fitting that an examination be made into what God's Words has to say on the subject of SEPARATION which is so important in the believer's life and the life of the church today.

   B.   **The Limitation Of The Problem.** By the very words "BIBLICAL TEACHING ON SEPARATION" there is implied that the study will be limited to the BIBLE treatment of the doctrine.

    1.   **Biblical Rather Than Theological.** The primary emphasis will be BIBLICAL rather than theological in the treatment of SEPARATION, though, of course, there is much that could be considered "theological" that will be brought into the treatment.

    2.   **Biblical Rather Than Contemporaneous.** Separation is an issue and a doctrine which is the main point of difference between such bodies as the NATIONAL ASSOCIATION OF EVANGELICALS (N.A.E.) and the AMERICAN COUNCIL OF CHRISTIAN CHURCHES (ACCC), for example. This is of current importance in America by virtue of the fact that these two great wings of conservative theology have been so at variance on the matter of SEPARATION, both from the NATIONAL COUNCIL OF CHURCHES, the WORLD COUNCIL OF CHURCHES, and even on the matter of SEPARATION personally from worldliness and sin. These details, though

they have been the subject of other publications of THE BIBLE FOR TODAY, will not be in primary focus in this study, but rather an analysis of the Bible on the theme of SEPARATION. Applications, of course, will be drawn from time to time to contemporaneous situations, but only incidentally.

    3.   **Biblical Induction To Be Relied Upon.** As the title would tell, this treatment of SEPARATION is primarily from a Biblical and expository viewpoint and as such is limited in general to an induction from the Bible of any and all of the verses that illustrate the practice of SEPARATION, properly arranged and expounded briefly. The treatment will therefore be Blbllcal rather than in the field of theology in general, practical theology, or contemporary theology.

    C.   **The Justification Of The Problem.** The fact that there are two wide factions in Conservative Protestantism is proof enough that the doctrine of SEPARATION is important. Though some Christian groups and individuals are not a part of either of the two warring factions, that is, either the NATIONAL ASSOCIATION OF EVANGELICALS (N.A.E.) or the AMERICAN COUNCIL OF CHRISTIAN CHURCHES (A.C.C.C.), nevertheless to the two groups doing battle, the problems of SEPARATION from apostasy and modernism which separate them, are extremely real and crucial.

    1.   **Questions To Be Answered.** Have the Words of God spoken in certain discoverable ways regarding the subject of SEPARATION? Has the Bible made it clear what is to be the Christian's stand on this issue? Does the Old Testament give to the church of today sufficient illustration of the doctrine to make it fit the times in which these groups (the NAE and the ACCC) are fighting about it? These questions are some that must be both raised and answered in the pages of this paper.

    2.   **The Relation Of The N.A.E. and the A.C.C.C.** Regarding the N.C.C. The two groups (the N.A.E. and the A.C.C.C.) vary in their opinions about joining in with the NATIONAL COUNCIL OF CHURCHES (N.C.C.). Up until 1950, it was called the FEDERAL COUNCIL OF CHURCHES. In all of their schemes. the NATIONAL COUNCIL is liberal in its doctrines and practices and is looked upon therefore as ungodly and diabolical in the eyes of the churches and groups making up the American Council of Christian Churches.

    a.   **The A.C.C.C. Position On The N.C.C.** The A.C.C.C. groups do not think that it is in accordance with the Bible to unite with the NATIONAL COUNCIL OF CHURCHES (N.C.C.) in a common cause, or for any other reason whatsoever, since it would be like uniting with Satan himself in a sense.

b. The N.A.E. Position On The N.C.C. The NATIONAL ASSOCIATION OF EVANGELICALS (N.A.E.), on the other hand, believes that this NATIONAL COUNCIL, though it is wrong in the main, is nevertheless a channel through which much that is good is being accomplished. It is possible, for example, therefore, to be a member of a church which is in the N.C.C. apostasy and at the same time be a member of the N.A.E. In fact, you can even be an important officer in the N.A.E., such as one of the Vice Presidents like G. Aiken Taylor, who was affiliated with the Presbyterian Church in the U.S. (Southern) which is in the NATIONAL COUNCIL OF CHURCHES apostasy, the WORLD COUNCIL OF CHURCHES (W.C.C.) apostasy, and the CONSULTATION ON CHURCH UNION (C.O.C.U.) apostasy!

II. METHOD OF PROCEDURE

A. The Statement Of The Method. The method that has been used in the preparation and presentation of this paper has been one of induction. This inductive method of taking all the particulars on any one subject and arranging them in order is the method used by men of science and even men of theology. Dr. Lewis Sperry Chafer, for example, used this inductive method to some extent in his eight volume *Systematic Theology*. He would read his Bible on the doctrine that he was writing on and then from the exhaustive commentary of Scriptures on this doctrine, he would begin to organize the doctrine for orderly presentation. Such an induction is the only method by which a thorough knowledge of any subject may be gained.

B. The Specific Method Used In This Paper. In preparation for the study of the "BIBLICAL TEACHING ON SEPARATION" the Bible itself was read over and over again, looking for but the one theme of SEPARATION in its pages. This data was then noted on special **Bible Induction Work Sheets** and placed to one side. Later on, these sheets were taken out and the various Scripture verses, numbering into the 100's, were looked up and classified in a general way. Actually, there were about 1,896 Bible verses in all.

1. Four Main Headings Were Found. These general classifications of the doctrine of SEPARATION were then arranged under four main headings and were allowed to rest again. After some weeks, the study was taken up again, this time by a re-reading of the Bible on each of the four main headings of the topic. The Bible verses were noted again on a separate **Bible Induction Work Sheet** in order to double check the previous work to make sure that most all of the verses bearing on that given phase of the subject were being taken into consideration. Since there were four main headings, the Bible was re-read four different times to double check each of these four main divisions to make sure that all the Scripture verses were noted in their proper order and under their proper division.

  2. **Scriptures Were Then Arranged Logically Under Each Of The Four Headings.** As a final step In the study, these individual main headings were examined as to the individual Scripture verses under each of them and were then classified and grouped in a logical way so that the chapters would be written about each of them. This, in brief, is the statement of the method used in the present study of separation. No outside books were used in arriving at the outline of the study, but the Bible alone told the story.

III. ORGANIZATION OF THE REMAINDER OF THE PAPER

A. **The Statement Of Organization.** The organization of the remainder of the paper will be as follows:

  1. **Summary Of Chapter Organization.** There will be a chapter on SEPARATION REGARDING THINGS, followed by one on SEPARATION REGARDING MARRIAGE, which will be followed by a chapter on SEPARATION REGARDING UNBELIEVERS. The final chapter in the body of the study will deal with SEPARATION REGARDING DISORDERLY BELIEVERS.

  2. **Chapter Two: SEPARATION REGARDING THINGS.** Chapter two will discuss under the general heading of SEPARATION REGARDING THINGS: (1) separation regarding natural phenomena; (2) separation regarding places; (3) separation regarding money or possessions; (4) separation regarding intoxication; (5) separation regarding specific sins such as (a) idolatry, (b) adultery, © covetousness (d) prostitution, (e) wizardry, (f) homosexuality, and the like; (6) separation regarding time; (7) separation regarding diet; (8) separation regarding Canaanite ways and doings, (9) separation regarding God's Words; (10) separation regarding animals, vegetables, and garments; and (11) separation regarding property.

  3. **Chapter Three: SEPARATION REGARDING MARRIAGE.** Chapter three will deal with SEPARATION REGARDING MARRIAGE. Under this heading, we will deal with the following subjects: (1) Dispensational aspects of marriage; (2) examples of separated marriages; (3) marriages with heathen; and (4) New Testament teaching on separated marriage.

  4. **Chapter Four: SEPARATION REGARDING UNBELIEVERS.** Chapter four will discuss the SEPARATION REGARDING UNBELIEVERS. The following subjects will be covered in this section: (1) Israel's separation regarding the Canaanites; (2) Failure in separation regarding

unbelievers; (3) success in separation regarding unbelievers; and (4) New Testament separation regarding unbelievers.

     5. Chapter Five: SEPARATION REGARDING DISORDERLY BELIEVERS. Chapter five will take up SEPARATION REGARDING DISORDERLY BELIEVERS. This is very much misunderstood in our days, and is sometimes called "secondary separation." Dr. John R. Rice, in his paper, *The Sword Of The Lord* has only recently come out as being definitely opposed to this sort of separation, claiming that the Bible did not teach it. In this chapter the following subjects will be dealt with: (1) Definition of terms; (2) Separation regarding orderly believers; (3) Old Testament separation regarding disorderly believers; and (4) New Testament separation regarding disorderly believers.

     6. Chapter Six: SUMMARY AND CONCLUSIONS. The final chapter, chapter six, will deal with a summary and some of the more important conclusions arrived at during the course of the paper.

     B. Justification Of Organization. Although there may have been other headings that could have been selected for the subject of SEPARATION as it is found in the Bible, the four headings of (1) THINGS, (2) MARRIAGE, (3) UNBELIEVERS, and (4) DISORDERLY BELIEVERS has seemed the most logical division. These headings also seem to me to be the most inclusive and crucial in regard to the entire concept of BIBLICAL SEPARATION, and were therefore chosen.

CHAPTER II
SEPARATION REGARDING THINGS

In the present chapter there will be discussed the general subject of separation as it pertains to various THINGS such as (1) SEPARATION REGARDING CANAANITE WAYS AND GOD'S WAYS; (2) SEPARATION REGARDING JEWISH CUSTOMS; (3) SEPARATION REGARDING MONEY AND VALUABLES; (4) SEPARATION REGARDING PLACES; and (5) SEPARATION REGARDING SPECIFIC SINS.

I. SEPARATION REGARDING CANAANITE WAYS AND GOD'S WAYS

A. Separation From Canaanite Ways. As Israel was to be separated from the sinful ways of the Canaanites, so the believers of this present age are to be separated from the evil ways of sin and Satan.

1. The Reason For Separation. When He called for SEPARATION of His people, Israel, from the sins and wickedness of the lands around about them, He had a special reason in mind.

a. Appreciation For God's Grace To Israel. God had given Israel a positional calling and election unto Himself and because of this, it was imperative that they separate themselves from sinful practices wherever they found them. It was God's grace that called them out of Egypt, from the house of bondage, and brought them into the land of Promise in Canaan. It was natural, because of this unmerited favor and grace, that Israel would want to give the Lord something in return.

b. God Wanted Their Bodies To Be Used For Him. The principal things that God demanded in absolute SEPARATION and consecration unto Himself, were the bodies of the Israelites, with all that this implied. The defiling of these bodies by desecration and debauchery was, in the sight of God, the highest type of sin and impiety.

c. God Wanted To Keep Pure The Messianic Lineage. God was looking for a people through whom He could bless the world by bringing the Messiah, the Lord Jesus Christ, from their lineage. If the line of the Messiah, who is called the Christ, were to be polluted by sin and dissoluteness on the part of the Israelites, God's plan would be thwarted. Satan was very much aware of God's plans, and made use of the Canaanites who were in such close proximity to the Israelites to tempt them through sinful pleasures and idolatry. This type of "wiles of the Devil" (Ephesians 6:11) whereby the believers of today are enticed to commit sin and thus lose their separated character is still present today. God wants a pure people, wholly separated from sin and unto Himself to the "praise of His glory" (Ephesians 1:12).

2. The Command For Separation From Canaanite Ways. In various places in the Bible, God gives the command to the Israelites to separate from the ways and doings of the Canaanites, in whose land they were dwelling.

    a. Leviticus 18:3, 24, 30. In Leviticus 18:3, 24, 30, God said:

After the doings of the land of Egypt, wherein ye dwelt, shall ye not do: and after the doings of the land of Canaan, whither I bring you, shall ye not do: neither shall ye walk in their ordinances. . . . Defile not ye yourselves in any of these things: for in all these the nations are defiled which I cast out before you: . . . Therefore shall ye keep mine ordinance, that ye commit not any of these abominable customs, which were committed before you, and that ye defile not yourselves therein: I am the Lord your God. (Leviticus 18:3, 24, 30)

This command is clear indeed. Egypt and Canaan both had defiled themselves with sin and God wanted the Israelites to keep away from any of this defilement.

    b. Deuteronomy 12:30; 20:17-18. In Deuteronomy 12:30 and 20:17-18, we are told:

Take heed to thyself that thou be not snared by following them, after that they be destroyed from before thee; and that thou enquire not after their gods, saying, How did these nations serve their gods? even so will I do likewise. . . . But thou shalt utterly destroy them; namely, the Hittites, and the Amorites, the Canaanites, and the Perizzites, the Hivites, and the Jebusites; as the Lord thy God hath commanded thee; That they teach you not to do after all their abominations, which they have done unto their gods; so should ye sin against the Lord your God. (Deuteronomy 12:30 and 20:17-18)

There is no hint of "dialogue" with these heathen unbelievers. Nor is the principle of "infiltration"(urged today by the so-called "NEO-EVANGELICALS") recommended for the Israelites.

    c. Other Scriptures. Though there are many other Scriptures pertaining to this particular point, the following will suffice to illustrate it more fully.

        (1) 1 Kings 14:24. This Scripture describes Judah's sins as being just like the heathen around them.

        (2) 2 Kings 21:9 and 2 Chronicles 33:2, 9. These verses picture Manasseh's sins as even greater than those of the people whom God had cast out from before them.

(3) **Ezra 6:21.** This verse shows how there were at least some of the Israelites who were obedient to God's Words and were SEPARATED from the sins of the Canaanites.

(4) **Ezra 9:1.** This verse shows how many other Israelites had failed to be obedient to God's command to SEPARATE from the Canaanites.

(5) **Ezekiel 11:12.** In this verse, God reproves Israel for acting like Canaanites. The warning against engaging in the sins of the people around us is a timely warning for today as well.

B. Separation Unto God's Ways. The positive phase of SEPARATION included being separated to the ways of the Lord. This plays an important part in the subject of SEPARATION--in fact it is of equal importance with the negative aspect.

1. **The Reason For Separation Unto God's Ways.**

a. **To Keep From Falling Into Sin.** God has always been a refuge for His people in times of stress, trouble, and temptations. If His people do not come to Him by reading His Words and by prayer in seeking His will for their lives, they might very well fall into the same sins of those around them.

b. **To Bring Their State Up To Their Standing.** God has already positionally separated and set apart His people to Himself. This positional setting apart or consecration by God argues for a practical living present reality in the life of His child. If the ultimate destiny of the believer is to be a 100% SEPARATION unto God and all that He is, what could be more fitting than for the believer to live a life in this world which is in dependence and trust on this One Who has loved him and called him unto Himself?

2. **The Command For Separation Unto God's Ways.**

a. **Some Of The Scriptures Listed.** The command for SEPARATION unto God's Words and ways as over against the keeping of the Canaanite statutes and ways is given in such Scriptures as: Leviticus 18:4-5, 26; 19:19a; 20:8, 22; 22:31; 25:18; 26:3; Deuteronomy 4:2, 9; 6:17; 10:13; 11:1, 18; 13:4; 26:16-17; 27:10; 30:16; 32:46-47; Joshua 1:8; 22:5; 23:6, 11; 24:24; Deuteronomy 17:18-20; 2 Samuel 22:23; 2 Kings 23:3; 1 Chronicles 28:8; 2 Chronicles 17:4; Ezra 7:10; Nehemiah 10:29; Psalms 1:2; 119:11; Jeremiah 7:23; 15:16; Acts 17:11, etc. Some of these are now cited more specifically as illustrations of the principle.

b. **Leviticus 18:4-5, 26.** God declared in Leviticus 18:4-5, 26:

Ye shall do my judgments and keep mine ordinances, to walk therein: I am the Lord your God. Ye shall therefore keep my statutes, and my judgments: which if a man do, he shall live in them; I am the

Lord. . . . Ye shall therefore keep my statutes and my judgments, and shall not commit any of these abominations. (Leviticus 18:4-5, 26) The positive walk by the child of God in God's Words is the best way to insure that there will be a negative SEPARATION also from sin. (Psalm 119:11)

  c. **Deuteronomy 4:2, 9.** In Deuteronomy 4:2, 9, we read:
Ye shall not add unto the word which I command you, neither shall ye diminish ought from it, that ye may keep the commandments of the Lord your God which I command you. . . . Only take heed to thyself, and keep thy soul diligently, lest thou forget the things which thine eyes have seen, and lest they depart from thy heart all the days of thy life: but teach them thy sons, and thy sons' sons. (Deuteronomy 4:2, 9)
Our children must be taught positive SEPARATION UNTO the Lord and His ways.

  d. **Joshua 1:8.** In Joshua 1:8, we are told:
This book of the law shall not depart out of thy mouth; but thou shalt meditate therein day and night, that thou mayest observe to do according to all that is written therein: for then thou shalt make thy way prosperous, and then thou shalt have good success. (Joshua 1:8)
SEPARATION unto God's Words carries the promise of His blessing and "prosperity."

  e. **2 Samuel 22:23.** In 2 Samuel 22:33, David could say:
For all His Judgments were before me: and as for His statutes, I did not depart from them. (2 Samuel 22:23)

  f. **2 Kings 23:3.** In 2 Kings 23:3, this principle is repeated again:
And the king stood by a pillar, and made a covenant before the Lord, to walk after the Lord, and to keep His testimonies and His statutes with all their heart and all their soul, to perform the words of this covenant that were written in this book. And all the people stood to the covenant. (2 Kings 23:3)
King Josiah pledged himself and his people to be positively separated UNTO the Lord and His statutes. This caused a revival in Israel.

  g. **1 Chronicles 28:8.** In 1 Chronicles 28:8, David told Solomon and the people of Israel:
Now therefore in the sight of all Israel the congregation of the Lord, and in the audience of our God, keep and seek for all the commandments of the Lord your God; that ye may possess this good land, and leave it for an inheritance for your children after you for ever. (1 Chronicles 28:8)

The keeping of God's Words insures an "inheritance" in the things of the Lord for our "children."

II. SEPARATION REGARDING JEWISH CUSTOMS

A. Separation Regarding Days. In the Jewish economy, there were certain days that were to be separated wholly unto the Lord. It is in the sense of consecration, dedication, and separation that such days form a part of our discussion of Biblical SEPARATION.

   1. Sabbath Days. In Exodus 20:9-11, the Sabbath day is mentioned. It was Saturday. The Israelites were to do no work on that day, since God rested on the seventh day of creation. Exodus 35:2 reiterates this sacred day, mentioning, in verse 3, that no fire was even to be kindled on that day.

   2. Feast Days. Leviticus 23 mentions seven feast days which were to be observed by the Jews, in addition to the weekly Sabbath day. These were: (1) The feast of Passover; (2) the feast of unleavened bread, (3) the feast of firstfruits, (4) the feast of Pentecost, (5) the feast of trumpets, (6) the feast of atonement, and (7) the feast of tabernacles. These were SEPARATED days, wholly unto the Lord to be used in a special way.

   3. The Day Of Jubilee. One other day set aside and wholly SEPARATED to the Lord was the day of Jubilee. This day occurred once every 50 years. On this day all the land went back to the owner who originally owned it. Leviticus 25 mentions the details of the Jubilee and gives the Jewish custom of reckoning prices from this day. It was a separated day unto the Lord.

B. Separation Regarding Diet. Since the Israelites were to be SEPARATED unto the Lord, even their diet was to be tightly controlled by the Lord.

   1. General Restrictions. Leviticus 11 and Deuteronomy 14 go into details of diet for the Israelites as none other verses do. Of the beasts that were upon the earth, the Jew was to eat only that which parted the hoof and chewed the cud (Leviticus 11:3). As for the fish in the sea, they were only to eat of those that had fins and scales (11:9). The fowls of the air are enumerated for the Israelites so there could be no doubt as to what was clean or unclean (11:13-19). It was clearly forbidden to eat any of the fowls that creeped, however. Creeping things of any kind were to be unclean to the Jew. By such a restricted diet, the Lord prevented many of the dreaded diseases that could have been carried by these unclean animals because of their inner make-up and their eating habits.

   2. Eating The Blood Forbidden. Though Saul seemingly did not take any care about the sin of the people in eating blood (1 Samuel 14:33), God

had nevertheless told His people that the blood was separated wholly to sacrifice and that it was a sin to eat of it. *"For the life of the flesh is in the blood: and I have given it to you upon the altar to make an atonement for your souls: for it is the blood that maketh an atonement for the soul."* (Leviticus 17:11)

Throughout the 17th chapter of Leviticus (cf. vv. 4, 10, 11, 12, 14) God warned His people against misusing the blood of animals. This typified the Blood of the Lord Jesus Christ, God's Son Who was to come.

    3. **Special Cases Regarding separation In Diet.**

        a. **1 Kings 13.** In 1 Kings 13, a man of God came out from Judah to pronounce a curse upon Jeroboam's altar. He was told by God (13:9) that he was not to eat anything while in the city of Bethel. He was therefore to be completely separated from food of any kind.

        b. **Daniel 1:8.** So in the case of Daniel 1:8. Daniel separated himself from the food of the king because of its evident pollution.

        c. **Romans 14:21 And 1 Corinthians 8:13.** Even in the New Testament (Romans 14:21 and 1 Corinthians 8:13), Paul suggested separation from certain foods offered to idols if it would give offense to weaker Christians.

C, **Separation Regarding Property.** Certain types of property were separated wholly to the Lord for some specific purpose in the Old Testament.

    1. **Property Separated Unto The Lord.** In Leviticus 27:14 and 27:22, both houses and fields were dedicated and separated unto the Lord. If the house or field were separated to the Lord, the price would be reckoned according to the day of Jubilee, and this amount would be given entirely to the Lord's work.

    2. **Separation Of Land To The Tribes.** After Palestine had been conquered by Joshua, the land was apportioned by him (Joshua 13-19) by separating districts for each of the tribes of Israel with the exception of Levi.

    3. **Levitical Cities And Cities Of Refuge.** Joshua 21 mentions the 48 Levitical cities taken from every other section of the land of Palestine, and separated for the Levites' special uses. From these 48 cities, six cities were separated from the others and called cities of refuge, where manslayers could flee until a trial could be held. Kedesh, Shechem, and Hebron were on the western aide of Jordan and Bezer, Ramoth, and Golan were on the east side of Jordan (Joshua 20:7-8).

> *These were the cities appointed for all the children of Israel, and for the stranger that sojourneth among them, that whosoever killeth any person at unawares might flee thither, . . .* (Joshua 20:9)

D. **Separation Regarding Disease And Sanitation.** Since sickness and disease was a very great problem to Israel, specially during wilderness wanderings, God made use of the principle of separation regarding disease and sanitation.

1. Separation Regarding Leprosy. In Leviticus 13 and 14, the principles of separation from leprosy were laid down in detail. The inspected leper appeared before the priest, and if found to be leprous, he was shut up and separated from the rest of the congregation to prevent contamination of others. This is a good illustration of how the believer today must keep away from sin and contamination. Even the clothes and homes were purified.

2. Separation Regarding Issues. This problem was dealt with in Leviticus 15. During the menstrual period, the women were to be separated and set apart. The same is true for other "issues" which some feel correspond to the venereal diseases of today. (cf. Leviticus 15)

3. Separation Regarding Corpses. In Numbers Chapter 6, the Nazarite (one who had separated himself from many things and unto the Lord Himself) was given specific rules. One thing he could not go near or touch, was dead bodies. He was to be separated even from his mother, father, brother, or sister if they had died (Numbers 6:6-7). Such restrictions were repeated elsewhere also. (Numbers 9:6; 19:11 ff.)

E. Separation Regarding Miscellaneous Customs. God so directed the lives of the Israelites that they were to do what He wanted them to do, even though the commands might have appeared foolish to them at the time. He wanted them to be separated unto Himself in trust and dependence.

1. Separation Regarding Mixed Animals. The Israelite was not to use both the ox (a clean animal) and the ass (an unclean animal) as a plowing team (Deuteronomy 22:10), nor was he to let his cattle gender with divergent kinds of breeds (Leviticus 19:19a). God even wanted the cattle and other animals to be pure, not mixed up. This is a clear lesson in principle for SEPARATION and purity before the Lord today.

2. Separation Regarding Mixed Seed. The Jew was to be separated in the sowing of his vineyard. He was not to sow different kinds of seeds in it (Deuteronomy 22:9). No field of any kind, in fact, was to be sown with different kinds of seeds, or mingled seed (Leviticus 19:19). Seed was to be kept SEPARATE.

3. Separation Regarding Mixed Garments. Even the Israelite's clothes were to be of a separated nature. He was to wear no mingled linen and woolen, for instance (Leviticus 19:19). This was repeated in Deuteronomy 22:11). Women were forbidden to wear that which pertained to a man and the men couldn't wear women's garments. To do so was, for the Israelite, an abomination to the Lord (Deuteronomy 22:5). I wonder what the Lord thinks of the so-called "UNI-SEX" garments conceived by the homosexuals who control the garment-making industry and designing in our world today? The priests of the millennial temple will be required to change their separated and holy garments to their common clothes when they finish their sacred ministry before the Lord. (Ezekiel 42:14). A SEPARATED walk, therefore, even extended to the Israelite's clothing.

III. SEPARATION REGARDING MONEY AND VALUABLES

A. Valuables Refused. God wanted believers to have a proper appraisal of valuables of all sorts. To SEPARATE oneself from valuables on certain occasions was to avoid grievous temptation and possible sin.

1. Valuables Refused By Abram. In Genesis 14, Abram recaptured Lot and the others in Sodom (that wicked city) who had been taken captives. The king of Sodom, delighted as he was to have all his people back to his city and to have the goods and treasures returned to the treasury, asked Abram if he wanted some goods as a reward (Genesis 14:20). Abram's answer indicated his SEPARATED character unto the Lord and from evil things:

... I have lift up mine hand unto the Lord, the most high God, the possessor of heaven and earth, that I will not take any thing that is thine, lest thou shouldest say, I have made Abram rich. (Genesis 14:22-23)

2. Valuables Refused By Elisha. Elisha also refused money on occasion. In 2 Kings, chapter 5, Naaman was healed of leprosy through Elisha the prophet of the Lord. (2 Kings 5:2, 14, ff.) Naaman offered Elisha money, but Elisha, the separated man of God that he was, replied:

As the Lord liveth, before whom I stand, I will receive none. And he urged him to take it; but he refused. (2 Kings 5:16)

3. Valuables Refused By Peter. In Acts 8, Peter and the other apostles were witnessing the blessings of the Lord upon them. Simon Magus was supposedly converted under the ministry of Philip (Acts 8:13). Simon Magus, having seen miracles done by Peter and John laying on their hands, offered them money for this gift. Peter not only separated himself from the money and refused it, he also said:

Thy money perish with thee, because thou hast thought that the gift of God may be purchased with money. (Acts 8:20)

Peter's refusal of the money, and his separation from it and all that it implied, was a badge of his separation to the will of God.

B. Valuables Separated For Special Use.

1. Money To Build The Tabernacle Separated For Special Use. In Exodus 35, the tabernacle was discussed by Moses. God commanded Moses to handle the financing of it as follows:

Take ye from among you an offering unto the Lord: whosoever is of a willing heart, let him bring it, an offering of the Lord; gold, and silver, and brass.... (Exodus 35:5)
This money and/or material was to be separated and dedicated unto the Lord by willing-hearted people.

2. **Firstfruits Separated For Special Use.** In Numbers 18, the Lord gave to the Levites the best of the oil, wine, wheat, and the firstfruits of all similar items. These things were separated wholly unto them (Numbers 18:12). The firstfruits also included the first of the corn, oil, and sheep fleece (Deuteronomy 18:4; cf. also Deuteronomy 26:2 and Ezekiel 44:30).

3. **Tithes Separated For Special Use.** The tithes (or first 10%) were to be the SEPARATED portion of the Lord Himself. They were to be used for the Levites and Priests since they had no inheritance with the other tribes of Israel (Numbers 18:24). These tithes were faithfully restored to the Levites under Hezekiah's reforms (2 Chronicles 31:12), but forgotten about in the time of Malachi (cf. Malachi 3:8).

4. **Valuables Presented To The Lord For Special Use.** After the slaughter of the Midianites in Numbers 31, the Israelites brought to the Lord a special offering, described as:

... what every man hath gotten, of jewels of gold, chains, and bracelets, rings, earrings, and tablets, to make an atonement for our souls before the Lord. (Numbers 31:50)

Such spoils of war were SEPARATED unto the Lord. Other instances of this kind of SEPARATION of valuables after wars are found in Joshua 6:19; 1 Chronicles 22:2-5; and 1 Chronicles 29: 2-3.

C. **Valuables Misused.**

1. **Multiplication of Gold And Silver.** Long before Israel had a king, one of the rules for kings was given in Deuteronomy 17:17b that a king should not multiply gold and silver unto himself. To use such wealth personally instead of presenting it to the Lord's house for repairs and needed expenses was a failure to separate the Lord's possessions unto Him.

2. **Multiplication Of Horses.** Since horses and cattle were used in Bible times in determining a man's wealth, as well as gold and silver, God was concerned with them. Since horses could be used for making war, God warned Israel against multiplying horses unto themselves (Deuteronomy 17:16). Solomon, however, failed to separate himself in this particular unto the Lord and thus multiplied horses freely in violation of God's Words (1 Chronicles 1:16; 9:25).

3. **Special Cases Of Misuse Of Valuables.** There are at least six special and notable cases in Scripture of the misuse of money or other valuables.

16   BIBLICAL SEPARATION   By Pastor D. A. Waite, Th.D., Ph.D.

        a.   1 Kings 15:18. Asa, in 1 Kings 15:18, gave the things of the Lord's house wrongfully to Benhadad in order to attempt to bribe him into being kind. Thus this wicked king of Syria became the recipient of the Lord 's gold and silver which had been SEPARATED wholly unto Him. Such sin was severely punished by the Lord.
        b.   1 Kings 20:7. In 1 Kings 20:7, Ahab, the King of Israel, gave his own money, to Benhadad, king of Syria, in order to make an alliance with him. Certainly a child of God's money has no business in the pockets of such a heathen king for the purpose of such an unholy alliance!
        c.   2 Kings 5:21-27. Gehazi, the servant of Elisha, committed the double sin of lying and theft by taking the money offered by Naaman which Elisha had refused (2 Kings 5: 21-27). Because of this mis-use of money, Gehazi became a leper as Naaman has been previously.
        d.   2 Kings 16:8. Ahaz took the silver and gold from the Lord's house, which had been consecrated to the Lord, (much like Asa had done in Judah), and gave them as a present to the king of Assyria. It was most unfitting to take the Lord 's money and give it to that wicked king.
        e.   2 Kings 20:13. King Hezekiah of Judah also committed the same sort of blunder regarding money when he showed the messengers from the king of Babylon all the gold and silver and precious things in the house of the Lord (2 Kings 20:13). These things were all separated to the Lord for His private use in the Temple.
        f.   2 Kings 11:1-16. Athaliah, the wicked female usurper, not only took money and valuables from the house of the Lord which had been SEPARATED unto Him, but she gave it to Baalim to further the worship of that pagan deity.

IV. SEPARATION REGARDING PLACES.

    A.   Separation Regarding Places To Leave.
        1.   Separation in Leaving Ur. Abraham was called of God to separate himself from Ur, his home, and go out to a place that God would show him (Genesis 12:1). Abraham had to be willing to SEPARATE himself from all his old ties in Ur. God had something better for him up the road of life.
        2.   Separation in Leaving Sodom. Lot, the nephew of Abram, was asked to SEPARATE himself from the wicked Sodom (Genesis 19). The angels' message, prior to the destruction of Sodom and the other surrounding cities, was one of SEPARATION. Lot had much invested in these filthy Sodomites and in the city of Sodom. He was reluctant to leave. So much so that the angels had to pull him by the arm (Genesis 19:16). Mrs. Lot died because she lingered and looked back longingly toward wicked Sodom. God

still had to get a lot of SODOM SEPARATED from Lot after Lot SEPARATED from the city of Sodom.

   3. Separation In Leaving Egypt. After Israel had been in Egypt for over 400 years, God's time had come for them to SEPARATE from it. God told Moses:

> *I have surely seen the affliction of my people which are in Egypt, and have heard their cry by reason of their taskmasters; for I know their sorrows;* (Exodus 3:7)

Later, the Lord further said to Moses:

> *And I am come down to deliver them out of the hand of the Egyptians, and to bring them up out of that land unto a good land* . . . (Exodus 3:8)

In order for the Lord to give Israel something far better, He first had to get them to SEPARATE from Egypt, which is a type of the world. Oh that believers today would profit from the application of this principle today! The world is too much present with us, in all of its filthy habits, customs, practices, and ways.

  B. Separation Regarding Places To Avoid.

   1. Separation In Avoiding Egypt. God had to remind Israel not to return to Egypt after He had redeemed them from it. In Deuteronomy 17:16, the future king was told not to multiply horses to cause Israel to return to Egypt. God said:

> *Ye shall henceforth no more return that way.* (Deuteronomy 17:16)

Isaiah (Isaiah 31:1) also warned Israel against going down to and trusting in Egypt. God wanted His people to be SEPARATED from and to keep away from Egypt.

   2. Separation In Avoiding Sinai. The Israelites were also to avoid touching Mount Sinai on the eve of the delivering the Law to Moses, God said to Moses:

> *And thou shalt set bounds unto the people round about, saying, Take heed to yourselves, that ye go not up into the mount, or touch the border of it: whosoever toucheth the mount shall be surely put to death:* (Exodus 19:12)

This SEPARATION from the mountain was a life and death matter. God also said to Moses:

> *There shall not an hand touch it, but he shall surely be stoned, or shot through; whether it be beast or man, it shall not live: when the trumpet soundeth long, they shall come up to the mount.* (Exodus 19:13)

Only when the trumpet sounded could they approach Mount Sinai, otherwise, it was off limits.

3. **Separation In Avoiding The Tabernacle.**
   a. **The Tabernacle In General.** The tabernacle was the place where God met with man in the Old Testament economy. His glory abode upon the mercy seat in the most holy place where the blood was applied each year, and where the cherubim stood vigil. Except for the high priest who entered through the veil once per year with the blood of the bullock for his own sins and the blood of the goat for the sins of the people, (Leviticus 16), this most holy place, or holy of holies, was SEPARATED from any other human being.
   b. **Uzziah's Violation Of The Tabernacle.** Uzziah, the king of Judah, failed to keep the holiest of all sacred, but entered the temple to burn incense unto the Lord without being a Levite or a Priest (2 Chronicles 26:16-21). For this violation of God's SEPARATION rules for the holy place, he became a leper unto his death.
   C. **Separation Regarding Places To Enter.**
   1. **Separation Regarding Entering Canaan.** In the Pentateuch, or first five books of the Bible, the land of Canaan was pictured as a land of opportunity and blessing. Canaan was a SEPARATED place into which God had planned His people to enter. It was a land "flowing with milk and honey." (Exodus 33:3).
   2. **Separation Regarding Entering Jerusalem,** The city of Jerusalem was a SEPARATED place where God could gather His people for His worship in the Old Testament. Even before Israel went into Canaan, God told Moses:

   There shall be a place which the Lord your God shall choose to cause His name to dwell there; thither shall ye bring all that I command you; your burnt offerings, and your sacrifices, your tithes, and the heave offering . . . (Deuteronomy 12:11)

   This practice made improper the heathen offering under every green tree in the high places. This is what made the altar of Reuben, Gad, and the half tribe of Manasseh on the other side of Jordan so wicked (Cf. Joshua 22). Jeroboam led his people into the sin of calf worship by failing to obey this rule of offering ONLY in Jerusalem (1 Kings 12:25-33).

V. SEPARATION REGARDING SPECIFIC SINS

A. **The Call To Separation From Sins.** God has issued many calls to SEPARATION from certain specific sins into which Israel was prone to fall. In Isaiah 55:7 and 59:2, God called upon Israel to forsake the wicked thoughts and ways and return unto the Lord. He mentioned that they had been SEPARATED from the Lord by their iniquities. Ezekiel warned the wicked to

turn from his evil way (Ezekiel 33:11), as did Zechariah some few years later (Zechariah 1:4).
  B. **Separation From The Sin Of Drink.**
    1. **Warnings To Separate From Drink.**
      a. **Warnings To The Priests To Separate From Drink.** In Leviticus 10, after Nadab and Abihu entered the tabernacle to offer strange fire on the altar which resulted in their deaths, God told Aaron:
      Do not drink wine nor strong drink, thou, nor thy sons with thee, when ye go into the tabernacle of the congregation, lest ye die: it shall be a statute for ever throughout your generations: (Leviticus 10:9)
Drunkenness was, evidently, the sin of Nadab and Abihu which led them to disregard God's regulations in approaching His tabernacle.
      b. **Warnings To The Nazarites To Separate From Drink.** The Nazarites also were to SEPARATE themselves from strong drink and unto the Lord. God told Moses, concerning the Nazarite:
      He shall separate himself from wine and strong drink, and shall drink no vinegar of wine, or vinegar of strong drink, neither shall he drink any liquor of grapes, nor eat moist grapes, or dried. (Numbers 6:3)
This abstinence from wine or the fruit of the vine was part of the Nazarite's vow. Samson's mother observed this vow because Samson was to be a Nazarite unto the Lord (Judges 13:3-5, 7, 14).
    2. **Examples Of Those Who Failed To Separate From Drink.** Israel did not wholly SEPARATE themselves from strong drink as God had commanded. They instead failed many times. Noah, Lot, and wicked Benhadad (1 Kings 20:16) fell into the sin of drunkenness. These individuals in the Bible who fell into drunkenness laid themselves open to all sorts of other sins while in their drunken state. Drunkenness was used of Satan to get Israel to commit sins of sensuality and idolatry (Cf. Provers 20:1; Isaiah 5:22; 28:7). Isaiah 28:7 mentioned that both prophets and priests have erred through strong drink, stumbling in judgment.
    3. **Examples Of Those Who Separated From Drink.** The Rechabites SEPARATED themselves from strong drink and were thus commended:
    Thus have we obeyed the voice of Jonadab the son of Rechab our father in all that he bath charged us, to drink no wine all our days, we, our wives, our sons, nor our daughters; . . . (Jeremiah 35:8)
  C. **Separation From The Sin Of Idolatry.**
    1. **Warnings To Separate From Idolatry.** In Genesis 35:2, Jacob had the revelation about idols and told his household:

Put away the strange gods that are among you, and be clean and change your garments:... and they gave unto Jacob all the strange gods which were in their hand, . . . (Genesis 35: 2, 4)

In the Law of Moses, God wrote:

Thou shalt have no other gods before me. Thou shalt not make unto thee any graven image, or any likeness of anything that is in heaven above, or that is in the earth beneath, or that is in the water under the earth: (Exodus 20:3-4)

These are only two of the many warnings against this sin of idolatry which the Lord gave to Israel, His idolatrous people.

    2. Examples Of Those Who Failed To Separate From Idolatry.

        a. Exodus 32. As early as Exodus 32, right after the Israelites had been redeemed from Egypt, and shortly after receiving the Ten Commandments from the Lord, they fell to worshiping images. Aaron was their leader in golden calf worship on this occasion.

        b. Leviticus 17:7. In Leviticus 17:7, God told Israel they were not to sacrifice to devils (and the images which were dominated by devils.)

        c. Judges 2:12. During the time of the Judges the evil of idolatry was extremely prevalent, as we're told:

They forsook the Lord God of their fathers, which brought them out of the land of Egypt, and followed other gods, of the gods of the people that were round about them, and bowed themselves unto them and provoked the Lord to anger. (Judges 2:12).

This idolatry and worship of Baalim, with all the vice this entailed, was hated by the Lord.

        d. Other Examples of Israel's Idolatry. There are many other occasions where Israel was guilty of idolatry in the Old Testament. Some of them were:

Genesis 35:2, 4; Exodus 20:3-4; 23:24; 32:2-4; 34:14; Leviticus 17:7; 20:2; Numbers 25:2-3; Deuteronomy 5:7; 7:25-26; 9:12; 12:2, 30-31; 13:6-8, 13-14; 16:21-22; 29:18; 31:16; 32:16-17; Joshua 23:7; 24:14; Judges 2:12-13, 17; 3:7; 8:27; 10:6, 10, 13; 17:3, 5; 18:30; 1 Samuel 7:3-4; 12:10; 1 Kings 9:6; 11:7; 14:23; 15:13-14; 19:18; 22:53; 2 Kings 1:2; 3:2; 10:29; 13:2, 6, 11; 14:24; 15:9, 24; 17:10-12, 16-17, etc.; 21:3-7, 21-22; 23:4-8; 2 Chronicles 25:14; 28:1-4, 23; 33:3-7, 15; 34:25; Psalms 78:58; 106:36; Jeremiah 9:14; 22:9; 32:35; 44:3; Ezekiel 8:14; 14:7; 16:1 ff.; 20:16, 24, 31, 23:1 ff.; 36:18; Daniel 3:12, 18; Romans 1:21, 23, 25; 1 Corinthians 10:14; Revelation 2:14; 20:4, etc.

D. Separation From The Sin Of Sensuality. God wanted His people to be SEPARATED from the sensual sins such as homosexuality, perversion of all sorts, adultery, prostitution, and the like.

    1. Warnings To Separate From Sensuality.

        a. Warnings To Separate From Prostitution. Leviticus 19:29 made plain God's desire for His people to be completely SEPARATE from the sin of prostitution. God said:

Do not prostitute thy daughter, to cause her to be a whore; lest the land fall to whoredom, and the land become full of wickedness.
(Leviticus 19:29)

This sin was prevalent among the heathen of that day, as it is today.

        b. Warnings To Separate From Homosexuality. When the angels of the Lord sought to bring Lot out of Sodom, they were surrounded by the Sodomites or homosexuals of the town who sought to have carnal relations with them. Leviticus 20:13 warned against this sin:

If a man also lie with mankind, as he lieth with woman, both of them have committed an abomination: they shall surely be put to death.
(Leviticus 20:13)

Many other places in Scripture forbade this same sin which is so prevalent today, and which is practiced by both men and women.

    2. Examples Of Those Who Failed To Separate From Sensuality.

        a. The People of Judah. Jeremiah warned that the people of Judah were as fed horses in the morning, *"every one neighed after his neighbor's wife."* (Jeremiah 5:8).

        b. Lot. Lot committed the sin of sensuality and incest as he allowed himself to become drunk and then to submit to sexual relations with his own daughters (Genesis 19: 35-36). There is no record of any repentance on the part of either girl for such wickedness, nor on the part of their father, Lot.

        c. Judah. Judah was taken in by the enticements of a woman and thus sinned by committing fornication with Hirah the Adulamite (Genesis 38:1-3).

        d. Other Examples Of Israel's Sensuality. There are many other occasions where Israel was guilty of sensuality in the Old and New Testaments. Some of them were:

Genesis 6:2; 9:22; 19:5, 8, 33, 35-36; 34:2, 7; 38:2-3, 14-15; 39:7-10; Exodus 20:17; 22:16, 19; 32:25; 34:16; Leviticus 18:6-23; 19:20, 29; 20:10-21; 21:7, 9, 14; Numbers 5:12-13; 25:1, 5-8; Deuteronomy 17:17; 22:22-30; 23:17-18; 27:20-23; Joshua 2:1; Judges 2:17; 19:22-25; 20:5; 1 Samuel 2:22; 2 Samuel 3:7; 6:20; 11:2-4; 13:11-14; 16:21-23; 2 Kings 23:7; 2 Chronicles 21:13;

Proverbs 2:16; 5:3-5; 6:24, 26, 32; 7:5-27; 22:14; Isaiah 1:21; 57:3; Jeremiah 3:2, 9; 5:7-8; 9:2; 13:27; 23:14; Lamentations 1:8-9; Ezekiel 16:15-63; 18:6, 11; 22:10-11; 23:3-49; 43:7-9; Hosea 1:2; 2:2-5; 3:1, 3; 4:2, 10-15, 18, Matthew 5:27-30, 31-32; 15:19; 19:9; Luke 15:13; 16:18; 18:20; 20:33; John 4:17-18; 8:3 ff., 41; Acts 15:20, 29; 21:25; Romans 1:26-27, 29, 31; 2:22; 7:3, 7-8; 13:9; 1 Corinthians 5:1, 9-13; 6:9,13-18; 7:2; 10:8; Galatians 5:19-21; Ephesians 2:3; 5:3, 5; Colossians 3:5; 1 Thessalonians 4:3, 5; Hebrews 13:4; James 2:11, 25; Jude 1:7; Revelation 2:14, 20-22; 17:2, 4-5, 15-16; 18:3, 9, etc.

CHAPTER III
SEPARATION REGARDING MARRIAGE

Having discussed SEPARATION regarding things, we now come to a consideration of the study of what the Bible has to say on SEPARATION REGARDING MARRIAGE. This chapter will take up: (1) The dispensational aspects of marriage; (2) examples of separated marriages; (3) marriages with the heathen, and (4) New Testament teaching on separated marriage.

I. DISPENSATIONAL ASPECTS OF MARRIAGE

A. The Dispensations Defined.

1. The Dispensation Of Innocence. The dispensation of Innocence had as its corresponding covenant the covenant made with Adam in Eden, and is hence called the Edenic Covenant. This rule of God on earth runs through Scripture from about Genesis 1:26 to 3:24. The duration of this age is not known, but it runs from the creation of man to the expulsion from the garden of Eden. As a result of man's failure in this dispensation, God pronounced a curse upon Satan, woman, man, and the ground. The Lord Jesus Christ is typically seen in the coats of skins used by God to cover Adam and Eve (Genesis 3:21).

2. The Dispensation of Conscience. The dispensation of Conscience had as its corresponding covenant the Covenant of Adam, or the Adamic Covenant. This age is described in Genesis 4:1--8:19, and lasted about 1600 years, from the fall of man to the flood of Noah. God judged man by a universal flood as punishment for his sin in this era. The Lord Jesus Christ is seen in the picture of the ark of Noah as it saved its occupants from death (Genesis 7-8).

3. The Dispensation Of Human Government. The dispensation of human government had the Noahic Covenant as its corresponding covenant. This age is described in Genesis 8:20--11:9, and lasted for about 400 years, from the flood to the tower of Babel. The confusion of tongues was God's judgment to mark the close of this era. The Lord Jesus Christ is seen typically in the burnt offering of Noah (Genesis 8:20).

4. The Dispensation of Promise. The dispensation of Promise was ruled under the Abrahamic Covenant. This dispensation runs from Genesis 12:1--Exodus 18:27, and lasted about 600 years, from the call of Abraham to the giving of the Law of Noses on Mount Sinai. The Egyptian bondage was the punishment marking the end of this age. The Lord Jesus

Christ is seen in the offering of Isaac (Genesis 22) and the Passover lamb (Exodus 12).

5. **The Dispensation Of Law.** The dispensation of Law was governed by the Mosaic Covenant. It runs in Scripture from about Exodus 19:1 to the death of the Lord Jesus Christ and lasted about 1500 years. The Assyrian captivity for Israel and the Babylonian captivity for Judah marked the judgment in this era. The Lord Jesus Christ is typically pictured in the five offerings (Leviticus 1-5).

6. **The Dispensation Of Grace.** The dispensation of Grace has a portion of the New Covenant and the Abrahamic covenant to govern it. The Scripture portion for this dispensation is Acts 2:1--1 Thessalonians 4:16, from Pentecost to the Rapture of the church. God will punish Israel and the Gentile nations in the Great Tribulation period to end this age. It has already lasted almost 2000 years and the Lord Jesus Christ is seen in the Scriptures which speak of Him (Luke 24:27).

7. **The Dispensation Of Kingdom.** The dispensation of the Kingdom will use the Abrahamic, Davidic, Palestinian, and New Covenants as its basis. This age is pictured in Revelation 19:11--21:1 and also in the Prophets and other portions. It will last 1,000 years and will end in the judgment of Satan's armies, Satan himself, and unbelievers of all ages. The Lord Jesus Christ will be seen then as King of Kings and the Great Judge (Revelation 19:16; 20:11).

B. The Dispensations Involved. The problem of SEPARATION regarding marriage is found only in five of the seven dispensations as it will be discussed in this chapter.

1. **Marriage In The Dispensation Of Innocence.** The marriage of Adam and Eve is basic to all understanding of marriage as it occurs elsewhere in the Scripture. A clear understanding of this portion helps to understand SEPARATION regarding marriage elsewhere.

2. **Marriage In The Dispensation Of Conscience.** The only problem text in the dispensation of Conscience is in Genesis 6, where the problem arises as to the identification of the "sons of God." The various views are given treatment in full by Keil and Delitzech, the Scofield Reference Bible, and Clarence Larkin's *Dispensational Truth*. Although I personally find Larkin's explanation the most satisfying of any, suffice it to say that there is a marriage problem in this dispensation, without going further.

3. **Marriage In The Dispensation of Promise.** In the dispensation of Promise, such men as Esau, Judah, Joseph, and Moses come up for discussion. In this era, then, there were more instances of the violation of SEPARATION in marriage than in the first two dispensations.

4. Marriage In The Dispensation Of Law. In the dispensation of the Law of Moses, the majority of instances of non-SEPARATION in marriage occur. Some of these examples come in the time of the wanderings, some in the time of the Judges, some in the time of the kings, and others in the time of the post-exilic writings.

5. Marriage In The Dispensation Of Grace. In the dispensation of Grace there are some apparent exceptions to the Scriptures implying SEPARATED marriage, and some Scriptures that demand SEPARATED marriage. This problem is not dealt with nearly so distinctly, however, in the age of Grace as is the case in the age of Law.

C. The Applicability of Separation In Marriage Teaching. It must be determined at the outset of this study what the applicability of SEPARATION regarding marriage can be in the various dispensations.

1. Marriage Occurred In Every Dispensation. It is clear that marriage has been going on from the dispensation of Innocence when God established it, and it will continue into the dispensation of the Kingdom until the eternal state causes it to cease.

2. Marriage Is Like Ethics. The institution of marriage is like ethics, that is, it has to do with what is right and what is wrong. It is a study in the realm of morals in other words. Just as murder was wrong in all the past ages, is wrong in the present age, and will be wrong in the future age of the Kingdom--so marriage in an improper manner is morally wrong no matter what the dispensation in question. This is our assumption at least.

3. Marriage Principles A Constant. Marriage principles are constant and do not change from dispensation to dispensation. So whatever may be the will of God concerning marriage in one age will also be the will of God in other eras on the same subject. Since marriage was instituted by God Himself in the garden of Eden and has been used as an illustration of the Lord Jesus Christ and the Church (Ephesians 5), it is hardly possible that its principles should be any other than constant and enduring. It is true, however, that God permitted a number of irregularities such as polygamy, divorce, and the like due to the "hardness of the heart" of men, but this was not God's BEST and directive will in the matter.

II. EXAMPLES OF SEPARATED MARRIAGES

A. The Lessons On Separation In Marriage From Eden. Since God Himself put Adam in the garden of Eden and brought the woman whom He had created unto the man and thus instituted the first marriage, it is important to note some characteristics of this first account.

1. **The Purpose Of A Wife.** Eve met a definite need for Adam and became his helper in life.

   a. **To Be A Helper.** When God had finished creating the great heavens and earth, with all of their parts, that is, light, firmament, dry land, sun, moon, stars, living creatures, vegetation, fish, and birds--He created the greatest of all creatures--man. Adam was the first man whom God had made from the dust of the ground, out of nothing. God had thought that one of the animals might be suitable as a helper to this man, but none of the animals qualified (Genesis 2:20). Woman was thus created to be that "helper" that Adam needed so badly.

   b. **To Meet A Need.** This part of the woman as being man's helper was part of the larger purpose for her creation--that of meeting his need. He needed companionship and fellowship. He needed someone to talk to. He needed someone also to produce after his own kind in the earth. All these things God provided for the man when He made Eve from his rib while he slept.

2. **The Nature Of The Wife.**

   a. **Eve Was Taken From The Man.** When God chose to set Adam on the earth, He did not make him from something of animal creation already in existence (as the false teachers who believe in theistic evolution teach), but He created him from nothing--using the dust of the ground alone. This was not, however, how He created Eve. He chose to take Eve from Adam's own rib, and thus to begin her existence. She was taken from the man, Adam.

   b. **Eve Was A Similar Creature To The Man.** We must assume that since she was taken from the man, Eve became a similar creature to Adam. She had the same number of teeth, hands, feet, toes, ears, eyes, and so forth. She had similar facial features, she lasted a similar number of years, she had similar brain structure and size, she was of similar stature and height. In short, with the exception of distinctive sexual differences, she was alike in almost every major respect to the man from whom she was taken. God saw to that.

3. **The Number Of Wives.**

   a. **The Word, "Wife," Is Singular.** The question often arises about God's ideal marriage. Is it monogamous or is it polygamous? Why did the patriarchs have more than one wife? Were they justified under the circumstances? Is this in keeping with the perfect will of God? It seems that the answer to all these questions is found in the singularity of creation here. God made only one wife to give to Adam--and no more! Thus it would be safely implied that He desired that it should always be so.

b. The Expression,"One Flesh," Is Singular. As further proof that God favored then and favors now a monogamous rather than a polygamous form of marriage, Moses used the expression "one flesh" to describe this Divine act of union in marriage. The Lord Jesus Christ adds an additional thought when He said that the two should be one flesh. (Mark 10: 7-9) This unity that has been thus achieved by the marriage of ONE man and ONE woman would be ruined if the ideal in marriage were TWO or THREE wives instead of ONE.

B. Examples Of SEPARATED Marriages.
1. Old Testament Examples Of SEPARATED Marriages.
a. The SEPARATED Marriage Of The Parents Of Moses. Though unnamed and often unsung, the parents of Moses stand out as towers in the plain of man's history because of their behind the scenes teaching of such a great leader of the people of God. In Exodus 2:1, they are not named [although later, they are called Amram and Jochebed (Exodus 6:20; Numbers 26: 59), in other sections of Scripture] but only called "a man of the house of Levi" and a "daughter of Levi." One thing is certain, however. In the midst of turmoil and trouble as captives in a strange land of Egypt, these two people remembered the laws of their God and married one another from the same tribe, instead of marrying one of the heathen Egyptians that were all around them. Thus these two Levites obeyed God and had an exemplary marriage and home. How our own believers need to heed such example today instead of marrying unsaved and heathen partners.

b. The SEPARATED Marriage Of Elimelech And Naomi. The case of Elimelech and Naomi is similar to the case of Moses' parents. They lived during the apostate times of the Judges when "every man did that which was right in his own eyes" (Judges 17:6) instead of doing the right and good thing in the eyes of God. Nevertheless they married each other as two Israelites both from Bethlehem-Judah (Ruth 1:1-2) instead of marrying someone from the heathen nations around them.

2. New Testament Examples Of SEPARATED Marriages.
a. The SEPARATED Marriage Of Zacharias And Elizabeth. In the days of Herod, the king of Judaea, a certain priest named Zacharias married a daughter of Aaron, whose name was Elizabeth (Luke 1:5). This illustrated the Old Testament pattern of marriage among the people of God as opposed to extra-Iaraelitiah marriages. Both were from the house of Aaron, the priestly family. They became parents of John the Baptist.

b. The SEPARATED Marriage Of Joseph And Mary. The marriage of Joseph and Mary is another example in the New Testament of a SEPARATED marriage. It says in Luke 1:27 that Joseph was of the house of David and if Luke 3 is taken to be the lineage of Mary, you have Mary as a direct descendant of David too, making their marriage one to the other on the basis of both being in the Davidic line. It was to such a home that God entrusted the human care of the Lord Jesus Christ, His Son.

c. The SEPARATED Marriage Of Aquila And Priscilla. It is said that Aquila was born in Pontus and came from Italy lately with his wife Priscilla because Claudius had commanded that all Jews were to leave Rome (Acts 18:2). This shows that they were both very likely Jews. Their hospitality, as mentioned by Paul, is understood when it is remembered that they had a Scripturally SEPARATED home in which love and Christian fellowship to all the saints could be nurtured without restraint. Such a Christian home should be the heritage of every believer today as well.

III. MARRIAGES WITH THE HEATHEN

A. Teaching Against Unseparated Marriages With The Heathen.

1. Teaching Against Unseparated Marriages By The Patriarchs. In Genesis 24, Abraham was an old man, well stricken in age, having been blessed by the Lord in all things. He called his eldest servant unto him and made him pledge something in regard to the marriage of his son, Isaac. Isaac was NOT to take a wife from the heathen around about him who were Canaanites, but was to go to his own kindred for his wife (Genesis 24:3-4, 37-38). Though it might be argued that these kindred in Ur of the Chaldees may have been pagans too, yet there is a possibility that Abraham might have witnessed to them of the true God and thus they might have received some of the truth of the one true God. If this was the case, the family would have been more reliable to pick a bride from than the families of the heathen nations around them. It is possible that racial reasons as well as religious reasons might have played a part of God's orders through Abraham to his son, Isaac.

Isaac did not fail to pass on this information to his favored son, Jacob. After Esau had taken a wife of the daughters of Heth, heathen Hittites of the land of Canaan, Isaac called Jacob unto himself and charged him not to do likewise, but to go back to Padanaram to his mother's father's house to take his wife. This he did, in obedience to his parents' wishes (Genesis 28:1-2, 5-9), with the testimony to it that even Esau his brother made an attempt to please his folks by marrying another wife of Ishmael's descendants.

2. Teaching Against Unseparated Marriages By Pre-Exilic Teaching.

a. Moses' Teaching To Israel Against Unseparated Marriages. After God renewed the covenant to Moses in Exodus 34, Moses began to speak to the Israelites regarding their position among the Canaanites among whom they soon would be dwelling. He explicitly told them NOT to take of their daughters for their sons nor in any way marry among these heathen people lest they teach idolatry to God's people (Exodus 34:16). So great was this teaching in importance that Moses repeated it to the next generation too. (Deuteronomy 7:3-4).

  b. Joshua's Teaching To Israel Against Unseparated Marriages. Joshua also mentioned this teaching about not marrying heathen to Israel after they entered the land of Canaan and toward the closing years of his life. He told Israel to love the Lord their God exceedingly so as not to make marriages with the heathen Canaanites who might then take away their heart from the LORD unto idols (Joshua 23:11-12).

  c. Samson's Parents' Teaching To Samson Against Unseparated Marriages. In the time of the Judges, there was also a clear revelation in the matter of SEPARATED marriages. Samson's parents (Judges 14:3) told Samson in clear language not to marry a woman in Timnath of the daughters of the Philistines whom he had come to "love." They asked him whether or not there wasn't a woman among the daughters of his brethren that he could marry instead of this pagan. Though the teaching on the matter was plain, Samson married her anyway.

  3. Teaching Against Unseparated Marriages By Post-Exilic Teaching. After the return of Israel from the captivity in Babylon, there was need for more teaching on the subject of SEPARATED marriages.

  a. Ezra's Teaching Against Unseparated Marriages. In Ezra's prayer to the Lord (Ezra 9:12, 14), he mentioned that God would not have His people take the sons and daughters of heathen people to be their husbands and wives. He reminded Israel that they should not repeat the sin of joining in affinity with the people of these abominations like they had done before God punished them in the captivity. He later called it a trespass and a transgression for an Israelite to marry a child of pagans (Ezra 10:10). Here again, the reason could have well have been racial as well as religious.

  b. Nehemiah's Teaching Against Unseparated Marriages. Nehemiah gave Israel more teaching against unseparated marriages (Nehemiah 10:30; 13:25). He made them make a covenant that they would not give their daughters to the people of the land nor take their daughters for their sons later in the book, he came right out and cursed and contended with them saying:

  Ye shall not give your daughters unto their sons, nor take their daughters unto your sons, or for yourselves. (Nehemiah 10:25).

  B. Reasons Against Unseparated Marriages With The Heathen.

  1. Reasons Against Unseparated Marriages That Concern God.

  a. So The People Would Not Transgress. The first reason that concerned God was the reason of transgression. Transgression or sin is violation of God's law and if there is sin in the relation of marriage, it is God who is hurt. This was the reason given against this practice in Nehemiah 13:27.

    b. **So The People Would Not Turn Away.** God wanted each of His people to love Him with a perfect heart, instead of loving some idol or some heathen practice. It was to safeguard this jealousy for exclusive love to Himself that God warned through Moses the future kings who would sit upon the throne of Israel. In Deuteronomy 17:17, the reason assigned for not multiplying wives unto himself (heathen wives is implied) is that his heart would turn away. This is the very thing which is said of Solomon (1 Kings 11:2-4, 9) who married so many ungodly heathen wives. They turned away his heart so that it was not perfect before the Lord his God. The Lord was angry with Solomon for this. (1 Kings 11:9).

    c. **So the People Would Not Be Idolaters.** God did not want His people to become idolaters. This explains the very first commandment of the Law of Moses. God alone was to be worshiped as supreme and His glory was not to be shared by another. This reason against marrying heathen is given by Moses (Exodus 34:16; Deuteronomy 7:3-4); by the writer of Judges (Judges 3:6-7); in the case of Solomon (1 Kings 11:2, 4, 7-8, 10); and in the case of Ahab (1 Kings 16:31).

    2. **Reasons Against Unseparated Marriages That Concern Man.**

    a. **So the Lord Would Drive Out The Canaanites.** In Joshua's closing words (Joshua 23:12-13), he mentioned mixed marriages with the children of Israel and the heathen. He indicated that if the Israelites followed the natural course of events and married the people who lived all around them instead of inter-marrying among themselves only in order to keep a pure stock of believers in the Lord, then the Lord would cease from driving out the Canaanites from the land as He had promised to do earlier. That would mean that the Israelites would have human leaders and armies, but no real Captain of the Lord's hosts to fight their battles for them. This would certainly restrict the area of land to be possessed by Israel's armies, and could work a hardship on all concerned. If they would only marry fellow-Israelites instead of pagan Canaanites, the Lord would continue the help and victories.

    b. **So The Heathen Would Not Be Snares.** In Joshua 23:12-13, God warned Israel that the heathen, if married, would be snares, traps, and scourges in their sides, thorns in their eyes, and that they would perish from off this land of Canaan. Heathen could be snares and scourges as well as thorns in many ways, and that would be manifested in every form possible of torment, morally, spiritually, sensually, politically, and idealistically.

c. **So Israel Would Be Blessed In The Land.** In the book of Ezra, the reason assigned for not making heathen marriages in the land of Israel, was that the people might be blessed in the land. Ezra wanted the people to be strong, to eat the good of the land, and to leave it for an inheritance to their children for ever (Ezra 9:12), and for that reason did not approve in the least of their inter-marriage with the pagans and other races of that day. Even blessing is dependent upon SEPARATED marriage.

d. **So The Israelites Would Speak Purely.** In Nehemiah's day, the Israelites could not understand their own brethren fully because of the inter-marriage with Ashdodites of the land, the Ammonites, and the Moabites. Marriage with these three heathen nations and races gave the Jews an impure speech so that Nehemiah said that:

... their children spake half in the speech of Ashdod, and could not speak in the Jews' language, but according to the language of each people. (Nehemiah 13:23-24).

The concern was for the content as well as the purity of the speech. This adds to the problems of inter-marriage, not only religiously, racially, but now even linguistically. All three considerations were made clear to Israel.

C. **Instances Of Unseparated Marriages With The Heathen.** Despite all of the Lord's warnings concerning the matter, Israel did have intermarriage with the heathen on many occasions.

1. **Instances Of Unseparated Marriages In-The Time Of The Patriarchs.**

a. **Esau's Unseparated Marriage With The Heathen.** Despite Abraham's clear teaching in regard to proper marriage (Genesis 24:3-4), Esau persisted in taking Judith, the Hittite for a wife, even though she was a grief of mind unto Isaac and Rebekah his parents (Genesis 26:34-35). This was not the end of Esau's disobedience in regard to an UNSEPARATED marriage, however, but in Genesis 36:2-3, three more heathen wives are listed as being Esau's: Adah the Hittite, Aholibamah the Hivite, and Bashemath the Ishmaelite (Genesis 36:2-3).

b. **Judah's Unseparated Marriage With The Heathen.** Even Judah, the head of the largest tribe in all of Israel, fell into sin when he left his brethren to go visiting with a certain Adulamite named Hirah. While there, he saw a Canaanitish girl named Shuah and married her, even though it was contrary to the known will of God as related by Abraham and Isaac years before (Genesis 24:3-4; 28:1, 6, 8; 38:1-2).

c. **Joseph's Unseparated Marriage With The Heathen.** Joseph sinned against God in the matter of his marriage, taking unto himself Asenath, the daughter of the heathen priest of On, who was the hand-picked choice of Pharaoh the pagan (Genesis 41:45). Such action would be justified by many today as being all right inasmuch as there were no other Israelites in Egypt, apparently. Could Joseph have refused the hand-picked bride of Pharaoh, his superior? The answer is that he could have thus refused this offer just as years before he had refused the offer of Potiphar's wife (Genesis 39:7-10). God's permissive will alone allowed Joseph to make this decision to marry Asenath, even though she is used by Bible students to be a type of the church.

  2. Instances Of Unseparated Marriages In The Time Of The Wanderings.
    a. Moses' Unseparated Marriage With The Heathen.
Moses was born in Egypt of two parents who were of the tribe of Levi. His mother had to forsake him when only a child, after nursing him for Pharaoh's daughter in his early years. Moses went into the Egyptian court as the son of Pharaoh's daughter, but when of age, left Egypt to dwell with the priest of Midian named Reuel. It was here in his household that Moses acquired his wife, Zipporah, who was definitely a pagan (Exodus 2:15-21). This is no doubt the same wife who was the subject of the complaint of Miriam and Aaron years later (Numbers 12:1). Thus Moses did not follow his good parents' example of SEPARATED marriage on religious grounds, and possibly on racial grounds as well.

    b. An Israelitish Woman's Unseparated Marriage With The Heathen. In Leviticus 24:10-16, an Israelitish woman married an Egyptian husband. This union was not blessed by God. After a number of years, this couple had a son who blasphemed the name of the Lord and cursed. This boy had to be brought to Moses to see what the will of the Lord was concerning him. Moses and the congregation of Israel, after knowing the will of the Lord concerning him (Exodus 24:13-14), carried out his punishment of death by stoning. This woman of Israel had taken the dread chance of marriage against the will of the Lord and was punished in the long run for it by the death of her blaspheming son who had no doubt learned such filthy and immoral language from his Egyptian father. The woman, Shelomith (Leviticus 24:11), surely committed sin with his unseparated marriage.

    c. Israel's Unseparated Marriages With The Heathen Moabites. After Balsam had been hired by Balak to curse the children of Israel (Numbers 22-24). Immorality, idolatry, and intermarriage with these pagans was common. It is said that the people of Israel began to commit whoredom with the daughters of Moab (Genesis 25:1) which meant in the marriage relation as well as the idolatrous relation which two things happened to be linked together in the worship of Baal-peor. So great was God's displeasure upon this sin of His people that he caused plagues to come upon Israel that caused 24,000 to die (Numbers 25:9).

3. **Instances Of Unseparated Marriages In The Time Of The Judges.**
   a. **Israel's Unseparated Marriages With The Heathen Canaanites.** In the days when the judges ruled in Israel, and when every man did that which was right in his own eyes, intermarriages with heathen people prevailed. A case to illustrate this is found during the time just before the Lord raised up Othniel to be the deliverer of Israel (Judges 3:9). The Lord had left some of the Canaanite nations in order to prove the children of Israel to see whether they would keep His way as their fathers did, or not (Judges 2:22). Joshua was dead and the Lord wanted to leave the remaining people to test Israel's true heart attitude toward Himself. So the Israelites dwelt among the Canaanites, Hittites, Amorites, Perizzites, Hivites, and Jebusites (Judges 3:5). Being among these heathen nations, Israel began giving their daughters to their sons and giving their sons to their daughters and serving false gods as well (Judges 3:6). Israel failed their test. Because of this failure, God showed His anger by selling Israel into the hand of Chushanrishathaim, the king of Mesopotamia, and made them serve for eight years.
   b. **Gideon's Unseparated Marriage With The Heathen.** After the writer of Judges described Gideon's idolatry, by making an ephod and an idol (Judges 8:24-27), he mentioned Gideon's married life. Gideon had a total of 70 sons born because of so many wives (Judges 8:30). One of his heathen wives was a Shechemite. From this marriage issued Abimelech the usurper who tried to be a king over the children of Israel (Judges 9:1-3) by killing Gideon's other sons. Such a pagan union was despised by the Lord.
   c. **Samson's Unseparated Marriage With The Heathen.** Samson has been much publicized because of his strength physically. But Samson had three pagan wives in direct rebellion to the will of God in the matter of marriage. The first wife was a Philistine who pleased him well (Judges 14:1-3) and who was hated by Samson's parents because she was a pagan. The second wife was a Philistine harlot whom Samson had desired in his lustfulness and departure from the Lord (Judges 16:1). The third pagan woman to darken the life of Samson was a Philistine from Sorek, named Delilah (Judges 16:4). She was the means of Samson's downfall and capture by his enemies, the Philistines. After putting him on her lap, she made him finally tell her where his strength lay; whereupon she had his hair cut off and his strength subdued (Judges 16:15-21). How much better off would it have been had Samson followed the advice of his parents and not married pagan women.

d. Naomi's Sons' Unseparated Marriages With The Heathen. In the time of the Judges, there was a famine in the land of Israel so Elimelech and Naomi, his wife, went into the land of Moab to sojourn until the famine was over. They took Mahlon and Chilion, their two sons, with them (Ruth 1:1-2). Since they continued there for some time, these sons married two Moabite women, Ruth and Orpah (Ruth 1:3-4). Instead of leaving this land and returning to Bethlehem-Judah, their home, they continued there 10 years, living in this pagan, wicked country of Moab. Elimelech and the two sons died soon after--perhaps as a judgment of God upon their Moabite sojourn and marriages (Ruth 1:3, 5). Even though Ruth is a type of the church, the fact remains that she was taken in marriage out of the will of God by an Israelite--however much in God's "permissive" will.

e. Boaz's Unseparated Marriage With Ruth The Moabitess. The marriage of Boaz with Ruth (Ruth 4:13), illustrates an unseparated marriage. Ruth was a Moabitess and Boaz was a kinsman of Naomi and therefore an Israelite (Ruth 2:1). Since Boaz was a kinsman of Naomi and Ruth's husband had died, it became the part of Boaz to perform the duty of marrying Ruth and raising up seed to her first husband who had died without any children. In doing this, Boaz forsook all the principles of marriage that God had before laid down clearly in His Words, since Ruth was a pagan woman. Again, God's permissive will is seen in His blessing of Boaz and Ruth in giving them children and finally in giving them as an ancestor, David, but the marriage was nonetheless wrong.

4. Instances Of Unseparated Marriages In The Time Of The Kings.

a. Solomon's Unseparated Marriages With The Heathen. Solomon's career of apostate marriages began with his marriage with Pharaoh's daughter (1 Kings 3:1), and was continued with his marriages of 700 wives and 300 concubines (1 Kings 11:3), who turned away his heart from the Lord and unto idols (1 Kings 11:4-8; 2 Kings 23:13). So notorious were Solomon's love escapades that he was used as an example of sin in the marriage relationship by Nehemiah (Nehemiah 13:26). In attempting to make alliances with all the nations of the Moabites, Ammonites, Edomites, Zidonians, and Hittites, he sinned against His God who had spoken to him concerning this matter twice (1 Kings 11:9-10). Solomon stands today as the greatest landmark of apostasy in unseparated marriage of any character in the Bible.

b. Ahab's Unseparated Marriage With The Heathen. Ahab sinned against the Lord in many ways. The root of his sin, however, was in his marriage to Jezebel, the daughter of Ethbaal, King of the Zidonians. Because of this marriage, his heart was turned to the worship of Baal (1 Kings 16:30-33). This woman was so wicked that she stirred up Ahab to work wickedness in the sight of the Lord, even to the selling of himself to that task in an all-out effort for evil (1 Kings 21:25-26). This woman, Jezebel, was so diabolical and wicked that even her murderer, Jehu, remarked about her harlotries and witchcrafts (2 Kings 9:22). Ahab's life was thoroughly ruined by the wrong choice he made when marrying wicked pagan Jezebel.

    c. **Jorum's Unseparated Marriage With The Heathen.** Ahab's son, Jorum, was reigning in Israel at the same time Jorum of Judah (sometimes spelled Jehoram) was King. This Jehoram, or Jorum, of Jerusalem, made the fatal and sinful step of marrying the daughter of Ahab and Jezebel and because of this, became a worker of all manner of evil in the sight of the Lord (2 Kings 8:16, 18). His wicked wife was thoroughly saturated with her mother's teachings of Baal and the other sins with which she was so adept. It was his wife, perhaps more than any other one thing, that caused the downfall of King Jorum of Judah.

    d. **Jehoshaphat's Unseparated Marriage With The Heathen.** It is mentioned in 2 Chronicles 18:1 that Jehoshaphat "joined affinity with Ahab." This Hebrew word translated "joined affinity" here is *yithchathen*, a hithpael third person masculine singular of the verb, *chathan*, which means "to mutually give and take daughters in marriage, to contract affinity by marriage." [B. Davidson, *The Analytical Hebrew and Chaldee Lexicon.* p. 280] So it seems that Jehoshaphat went to the house of wicked Ahab, who himself was already steeped in heathen marriage, to get a wife, instead of following the Lord's will in this matter.

    e. **Three Evil Mothers' Unseparated Marriage Ideas.** It is of interest to note that three wicked mothers are mentioned in Scripture, each of which was married contrary to the Words of God to one of the kings of either Judah or Israel:

    (1) **Naamah**, the Ammonitess, mother of Rehoboam and wife of Solomon (1 Kings 14:31).

    (2) **Maachah**, the mother of Abijam and wife of Rehoboam (1 Kings 15:2; 2 Chronicles 15:16).

    (3} **Athaliah**, mother of Ahaziah and wife of Jehoram of Judah (2 Kings 8:26; 11:1; 2 Chronicles 22:2-3). All of these evil women were improperly married to an Israelite.

   5. **Instances Of Unseparated Marriages in the Time of the Post-Exile.**

    a. **Ezra's People's Unseparated Marriages With The Heathen.** After Ezra had led some of the people of God back from their captivity they began once again to inter-marry with the daughters of the land, marrying Canaanites, Hittites, Perizzites, Jebusites, Ammonites, Moabites, Egyptians, and Amorites (Ezra 9:1-2). This became a sin unto them and after

Ezra preached against it (Ezra 9:12, 14), they began to mourn over their actions (Ezra 10:1-2). The result of this godly sorrow was a covenant not to again do this thing (Ezra 10:3). So great had the evil influence of heathen marriage reached that many of the priests had been found with strange, unseparated wives (Ezra 10:18).

          b. **Nehemiah's People's Unseparated Marriages With The Heathen.** Nehemiah also had this trouble with his people that he brought up from the captivity of Babylon and Assyria (Nehemiah 13:23-30). The Jews had married the people of Ashdod so that they could not even understand all their speech (Nehemiah 13:23-24). The most notable example of sin in regard to heathen marriage was Joiada, the son of the high priest, who had evidently married Sanballat the Horonite's daughter (Nehemiah 13:28). Nehemiah was much concerned about the defilement of the priesthood and of the Levites by this sin against God (Nehemiah 13:29), but God was even more concerned because it was His law that they had violated in their sinful, unseparated marriages.

          c. **Esther's Unseparated Marriage With The Heathen.** Esther 2:17 describes the marriage of the Jewess, Esther, to the heathen and extremely wicked king, Ahasuerus. This fact of illicit and illegal marriage between Ahasuerus and Esther is not very often brought out by commentators and preachers from the book of Esther. It is nevertheless present. While it is true that Esther was seemingly brought to the throne for "*such a time as this*" to save the Jewish nation from being annihilated by Haman, this must be relegated to God's permissive will in the matter (rather than directive will), because of the outright sin against the clear teachings of God that was committed by Esther when marrying this pagan king. Her marriage was further rendered sinful and corrupt by the way in which it was brought about (Esther 2:12-17).

IV. NEW TESTAMENT TEACHING ON SEPARATED MARRIAGE

    A. Apparent Exceptions To Separated Marriage.
        1. **1 Corinthians 7, As An Apparent Exception To Separated Marriage.** In 1 Corinthians 7, Paul explains the whole relationship of Christian marriage.

            a. **The Need For Marriage.** He starts by explaining that there is need for marriage for all who would otherwise be tempted to commit the sin of fornication (1 Corinthians 7:1).

            b. **The Marital Duties Of Husbands And Wives.** Paul next takes up the marital duties of both husband and wife in the marriage relation. (1 Corinthians 7:3-5).

c. **Widows, Bachelors, And Separations.** Then, after talking briefly about widows and bachelors and separations of husband and wife, Paul mentions the case of a woman which has an unbelieving husband (1 Corinthians 7:13-16). This case is prefaced by a short word about a husband having an unbelieving wife (1 Corinthians 7:12).

d. **The Case Of A Man Having An Unbelieving Wife.** In the case of a man having an unbelieving wife, it must be understood that both of the partners were unsaved when they married, but since their marriage, one of them, the husband in this case, had believed on the Lord Jesus Christ and had thus become a believer. The case of the woman having an unbelieving husband is similar.

e. **The Case Of A Woman Having An Unbelieving Husband.** In 1 Corinthians 7:13-16, the case of the woman having an unbelieving husband is taken up. The wife had been converted since their marriage, and she was to stay with her unsaved husband instead of deserting him. This way he might accept the Lord Jesus Christ as Savior and thus re-united their home.

f. **1 Corinthians 7 NOT An Exception To The SEPARATED Marriage Rule At All.** So, though 1 Corinthians 7 seems to speak about a believer marrying an unbeliever, to the contrary, it gives practical teaching to those whose homes have been divided since marriage by one becoming a Christian and the other remaining in his or her unsaved state. The present tense of the verb translated "hath" in the phrase "hath a wife that believeth not" (1 Corinthians 7:12) is decisive on the fact that the wife had the husband for a long time and since that time had become converted by the preaching of Paul or some other believer. [Cf. A. T. Robertson, *Grammar of the Greek New Testament In The Light Of Historical Research*, pp. 879 ff.]

2. **1 Peter 3, As An Apparent Exception To Separated Marriage.**

a. **The Problem.** The passage in 1 Peter 3:1-6 is likewise an apparent exception to the rule of marriage with believers only. Peter exhorts the wives to be in subjection to their own husbands that if any of them obeyed not the Words of God they may be won without a single word from them as they behold their chaste and holy manner of life.

b. **Two Possible Explanations.**

(1) **Possibly A Disobedient Christian Is In Mind.** The first explanation is that the meaning of the phrase, "if any obey not the word" is merely that the husband is a disobedient Christian, not necessarily an unbeliever.

(2) **Possibly A Marriage When Both Were Unsaved.** A second explanation is that the meaning of the phrase, "if any obey not the

word is that the man is an unbeliever, but that when the wife married him, they were BOTH unsaved (as in 1 Corinthians 7 above), but since that time she has become a Christian and now has the task of trying to lead him to the Lord Jesus Christ. This would be in line with the passage in 1 Corinthians 7. Regardless as to which explanation of the case in question is taken, it is certainly true that the meaning must necessarily be that a believer is married to an unbeliever.

    B.   **Scriptures Implying Separated Marriage.**
        1.   **1 Timothy 3:11 Implies SEPARATED Marriage.** In the catalog of qualifications required for the deaconate in 1 Timothy 3:8-13, there is mentioned that the wives of the deacons must be grave, sober, faithful in all things and not slanderers (1 Timothy 3:11). This is necessarily an implication that the wives of deacons must be believers, for in no other way could they be "faithful in all things" than first to believe on the Lord Jesus Christ as their personal Savior.

        2.   **1 Peter 3:7 Implies SEPARATED Marriage.** In 1 Peter 3, there is also an implication that men are to be married to believing wives. In verse 7, the husbands are to dwell with the wives according to knowledge, giving honor unto them as weaker vessels and heirs together of the grace of life. This heirship may refer to the grace of eternal life and hence there is an implication that both must be believers. Then the phrase "that your prayers be not hindered" (1 Peter 3:7b) would bear this out also, that is, that the couple would both be believing Christians.

        3.   **2 Corinthians 6:14-18 Implies SEPARATED Marriage.** While by no means being the only teaching involved in 2 Corinthians 6:14-18, or even being the main teaching, nevertheless the subject of marriage with heathen unbelievers in the New Testament is clearly implied in this passage. When Paul said that the Corinthian believers were not to be unequally yoked together with unbelievers, he included the marriage relation too. The marriage bond is considered a yoke, and if one person is a believer and the other is an unbeliever, that yoke is "unequal" and is therefore against the will of God. Though there are many preachers that think it is all right to marry believers with unbelievers or with professed believers who are questionable, the teaching of the Words of God through Paul is clear that believers are to marry only other believers in order that the home might be truly Christian.

    C.   **Scriptures Demanding Separated Marriage.**
        1.   **Ephesians 5:22-33 Demands SEPARATED Marriage.** In this section of the Scripture, Paul puts forth the teaching on the Christian home.
            a.   **The Background.** Paul demands of husbands that they love their own wives as the Lord Jesus Christ loved the church. To the wives, he writes that they subject or submit themselves to their own husbands as unto the Lord. This certainly would have very little meaning unless both man and

wife were true believers and were thus made alive to God and to the Lord Jesus Christ by faith in the Son.

  b. The Verses Could Not Be Fulfilled If An Unseparated Marriage Were In View. How could it be possible for the wife to submit as unto the Lord Jesus Christ (Ephesians 5:22) unless she had known Him as her Savior? How could it be intelligent to assume that a husband could love his own wife as the Lord Jesus Christ loved the church and gave Himself for it unless that husband were born again by the Spirit of God and thus acquainted with the price of his redemption and the great love wherewith the Lord Jesus Christ loved him? It seems incredible that Paul would be assuming any other state to be true than for the wives and husbands both to be believers in this context.

  c. The Analogy Of Christ And The Church. Further on in the context of Ephesians 5, the Church and the Lord Jesus Christ sustain a relationship as do a bride and her bridegroom, or as a wife and her husband. Paul taught that the Lord Jesus Christ loved the Church and gave Himself for it that He might present it unto Himself as a glorious church, without spot or wrinkle or any such thing. Then Paul mentioned that the church should be holy and without blemish as a result of Christ's love for it. Thus there is a divine analogy between marriage and salvation.

  d. This Analogy Could Not Be Used If Not A SEPARATED Marriage In View. Could this analogy be used with any degree of correctness and propriety if it were God's will for believers in this age, or any other age, to marry unbelievers? Could the Lord Jesus Christ be likened to the husband if that husband were ungodly and lost in trespasses and sins? Could the glorious redeemed church universal be illustrated by a wife or a bride if that wife or bride were an unsaved wench who had not known the saving power of God? Of course not. In order for this illustration to carry any weight and to have any importance, it must be true that God's ideal picture of marriage is for the believer to marry a believer, even as in the garden of Eden, Adam married a like creature who was sympathetic to his needs.

  e. This Analogy Tends To Prove Marriage Principles Are Unchangeable. This analogy further proves that marriage principles are as eternal as the thought of the Lord Jesus Christ and the Church in the mind of God, and are not, therefore, changeable from dispensation to dispensation.

  2. Revelation 19:7-9 Demands SEPARATED Marriage. In the 19th chapter of Revelation, verses 7-9, John is describing the marriage supper of the lamb.

  a. The Setting. There is the call for rejoicing because the marriage of the Lamb is come and His wife has made herself ready. This wife was arrayed in the finest of linen, clean and white, which symbolizes the righteousnesses of the saints (Revelation 19:8). The picture is of the Lord Jesus Christ and the bride which is the church dining together before the marriage proper.

    b. The Church Has Been Raptured. The church had already been raptured by this time and had received the new bodies like unto His glorious body (Philippians 3:20-21), and had gone through the cleansing and purifying ordeal of the judgment seat of Christ (2 Corinthians 5:10) at which place each believer was judged for the things done in the body according to that which he had done (2 Corinthians 5:10). Now comes the final event that came before the marriage itself, that is, the marriage supper which fitted perfectly the order of Jewish tradition.

    c. The Bride Could Not Be Unsaved and UNSEPARATED. Could the bride and wife-to-be be a picture of an unbeliever in the marriage relation? Is it conceivable that the Lord Jesus Christ should spend all eternity--world without end--with the church, His bride and wife, when that bride typifies the relationship of marriage which could allow union between believer and unbeliever alike? Certainly not.

    d. This Passage Illustrates God's Ideal Of SEPARATED Marriage. This passage, along with Ephesians 5:22-33, serves all the more to prove that God's picture of ideal, Heavenly marriage is a picture which precludes any non-separated marriage union between heathen pagans and believers in relationship with God. It is seen, therefore, that the New Testament teaching on SEPARATED marriage stands united with the Old Testament teaching on this same truth.

CHAPTER IV
SEPARATION
REGARDING UNBELIEVERS

The present chapter follows that on marriage in logical order. Since unbelievers are involved in marriages of an UNSEPARATED variety, as well as in many other things to be discussed in this division of the study. Though separation regarding marriage, in reality, belongs to the present chapter, since it was such an extended subject in itself that it was considered in a separate section. The present chapter divides itself into the following divisions: (l) Israel's SEPARATION regarding the Canaanites; (2) failure in SEPARATION regarding unbelievers; (3) success in SEPARATION regarding unbelievers, and (4) New Testament SEPARATION regarding unbelievers.

I. ISRAEL'S SEPARATION REGARDING THE CANAANITES

A. Separation Teaching Regarding The Canaanites.
   1. The Canaanites Were To Be Removed.
      a. **The Remover Of The Canaanites**. In all of the teaching to Israel regarding the Canaanites, God is spoken of as being the Remover of these wicked people from their land (Deuteronomy 7:19-21; 9:3; 11:25; 12:29; 19:1; 31:6; Joshua 3:10; 23:3, 5, 9-10). Though human leaders were to be used, nevertheless it was God or God's Angel (Exodus 33:2) Who was to do the actual removing of these unbelievers from the promised land.
      b. **The Reason For The Removal Of The Canaanites**. The reason for the removal of the unbelieving Canaanites was the promise of God to Abraham (Genesis 15:16) that he should return to that land later because the iniquity of the Amorites had not yet been filled. The sins of the people of the land became the superficial factor, other than God's promise, in their removal, not the inherent goodness of Israel (Deuteronomy 9:4-6).
      c. **The Method Of Removal Of The Canaanites**. So sinful were these unbelievers who inhabited the land of Canaan that God was to remove them either by driving them out of the land (Exodus 33:2; Numbers 33:52; Deuteronomy 7:1; 9:3b; 11:22-24; Joshua 3:10; 23:5), or by destroying them by death (Exodus 23:23; Deuteronomy 7:2, 16, 20, 23-24; 9:3b; 12:29; 19:1; 20:16-17; Joshua 11:20). In either case, the Canaanites were to have been removed from the land of Canaan which God had given to His people Israel as an inheritance promised years before to Abraham their father after the flesh.

2. **Israel's Instructions Regarding SEPARATION From The Canaanites.**

a. **Separation From Canaanites Regarding Covenants.** Moses was clearly warned against making a covenant with any of the inhabitants of the land into which he was to one day go so that they would not be a snare unto the Israelites (Exodus 34:12). This warning was repeated over and over again to Moses and to the Israelites (Exodus 34:12; Deuteronomy 7:2, 16b; 20:10, 16; Joshua 11:20) so that no nation would come out against Israel with the intention of making a truce or a peace with them. This would make it humanly impossible to destroy them or otherwise remove them from their land.

b. **SEPARATION From Canaanites Regarding Fellowship.** Israel was also warned against making any fellowship of an intimate sort with the Canaanites either in a personal way (Joshua 23:7, 12), or regarding any of their sins (Leviticus 18:3-4, 24-30; Deuteronomy 18:9-10; 20:18). Being in such close contact with these sinful people, it was naturally hard for the Israelites to abstain from either personal fellowship or fellowship in the ways of the Canaanites, but this is given in the Scriptures as the will of God. In this respect. Israel was a SEPARATED and a set-apart people and should have acted like it. We today who are believers in the Lord Jesus Christ, are to maintain a SEPARATED walk in the midst of all our "Canaanites" in the world around us as well.

c. **SEPARATION From Canaanites Regarding Marriage.** This subject has been discussed above in Chapter III, but it is important in this section as well. As Moses was repeating to the new generation of Israelites that had grown up while in the wilderness, he mentioned the Angel of the Lord would go before them and drive the nations of the Hittites, Girgashites, Amorites, Canaanites, Perizites, and Hivites out of the land, as well as the other heathen nations; even though these nations were greater and mightier than Israel (Deuteronomy 7:1). Then he gave orders to smight them in such a way as to destroy them, making no covenant with them nor taking any of their daughters to be wives unto the Israelites so that their hearts would not be turned away (Deuteronomy 7:2-4).

d. **SEPARATION From Canaanites Regarding Idolatry.** As further instructions for the children of Israel as they marched into the land of Canaan, God told them not to take up with any of the heathen idols worshiped by the heathen in the land, but He told them to destroy their altars, break down their images, and cut down their idolatrous groves (Exodus 34:13; Numbers 33:52; Deuteronomy 7:5, 25; 12:2-3). In no real way were God's own chosen people to be united in a common bond of worship with the unclean, unbelieving people that were then dwelling in the land of Canaan. This should be true of the Christian believers today as well!

B. Obedience To The SEPARATION Teaching Regarding The Canaanites.

1. Obedience To The SEPARATION From Canaanites in the Time Of Moses.

a. SEPARATION From Sihon. As the Israelites, under the noble leadership of Moses, marched from Egypt through the wilderness and into the general area of the promised land, they met with opposition from Sihon, King of Heshbon. The children of Israel wanted to pass through the Amorite's coasts (Deuteronomy 2:27), but Sihon would not tolerate this (Deuteronomy 2:30). This was all of the Lord so that Israel could meet this wicked nation in battle and destroy them (Deuteronomy 2:24-25). So Moses, in obedience to God, took all Sihon's cities and utterly destroyed all the men, women, and children (Deuteronomy 2:34). This event has been noted in other places in Scripture also (Cf. Deuteronomy 31:4; Joshua 24:12).

b. SEPARATION From Og. After Israel had battled Sihon, they came to the land of Bashan where Og was king. Og had come out against Israel in full battle array when the voice of the Lord spoke peace to Moses' fearful heart. God said:

Fear him not; for I will deliver him, and all his people, and his land, into thy hand; and thou shalt do unto him as thou didst unto Sihon king of the Amorites, . . . (Deuteronomy 3:2).

God indeed kept His promise and Moses and the people succeeded in utterly destroying Og and all his people (Deuteronomy 3:3, 6).

2. Obedience To The SEPARATION From Canaanites In The Time Of Joshua. Success in obedience to God's Words in driving out the inhabitants of the land was also in evidence in the time of Joshua. It is recorded that Joshua and all the men of Israel fought against Debir (Joshua 10:38) and defeated it, smiting all the cities surrounding this territory with the sword and utterly destroying all the souls therein. Though this seems hard for a New Testament believer to understand, yet in God's will and way, it was a method of meting out judgement to these unbelievers who had rejected the light of God (Joshua 10:39-40). In this respect it is similar to God's eternal, everlasting Hell fire. It is recorded that Joshua did not make peace with any nation that he went into with the exception of Gibeon (Joshua 11:19) because the Lord hardened the hearts of the people that they should come out against Israel so God could defeat them (Joshua 11:20).

C. Disobedience To The SEPARATION From Canaanites.

1. Disobedience To SEPARATION Regarding Their Removal. Even in the time of Joshua it is recorded that the children of Israel failed to expel the Geshurites and the Maachathites (Joshua 13:13). This is one of many instances of failure to obey completely the Words of the Lord in the treatment of these unbelievers (Cf. Joshua 17:12; Judges 1:21, 27, 29, 30-34; 1 Kings 9:20-21; 2 Chronicles 8:7-8).

    2.   **Disobedience To SEPARATION Regarding Covenants**. The Gibeonites deceived the children of Israel into thinking that they were from the East side of Jordan or at least from a far distant land and thus made a covenant with Israel contrary to the will of God (Joshua 9:6, 7, 15-16; 11:19). This was not the only covenant made with heathen in disobedience to the Words of God, but it is the main one (Cf. Judges 2:2; 1 Kings 9:21).

    3.   **Disobedience To SEPARATION From Canaanites Regarding Fellowship**. The Israelites broke their SEPARATION regarding fellowship in the ways of the heathen Canaanites also as is recorded in 2 Kings 17:8 and also in Psalm 106:35 ff. The Israelites failed to keep away from fellowshipping with the Canaanites but continued to practice some of their evil ways after making covenants with them and allowing them to live.

    4.   **Disobedience to SEPARATION Regarding Marriage**. God had warned Israel against intermarriage with the heathen many times, but His warnings were unheeded in numerous cases as has been brought out in the previous chapter (Cf. Chapter III above).

    5.   **Disobedience To SEPARATION From Canaanites Regarding Idolatry**. True SEPARATION from unbelievers as God had commanded Israel with regard to the Canaanites demands also a SEPARATION from their sinful practices such as idolatry. This was not followed, however, as is brought out in the chapter describing the reason God took Israel into captivity (Cf. 2 Kings 17:33). It is said that they feared the Lord in a half-hearted sort of way, yet served their own gods, after the manner of the nations which they had previously tried to expel from the land. This fact is also noted in the historical Psalm that recalled the history of Israel (Psalm 106:36 ff.):

> *They served their idols: which were a snare unto them* . . . (Psalm 106:36).

II. FAILURE IN SEPARATION REGARDING UNBELIEVERS IN GENERAL

    A.   **Failure in SEPARATION With Unbelievers In The Time Of The Patriarchs.**

    1.   **Abram's Failure In SEPARATION From Unbelievers**. In Genesis 12, Abram and his wife, Sarai, went down into the land of Egypt to sojourn during a famine (Genesis 12:10). While there, instead of taking a resolute stand of SEPARATION regarding these Egyptians and letting them know that Abram knew the Lord God, he cringed and cowered with fear--even denying that Sarai was his wife, lest the Egyptians might kill him in order to

take her for themselves (Genesis 12:11-16). He made her say she was only his sister, for the sake of advantage for himself. He repeated this compromising later also (Genesis 20:2).

2. **Lot's Failure In SEPARATION From Unbelievers.**

a. **Lot's Failure In SEPARATION By His Choice Of Sodom.** Lot had no right or business to choose Sodom to stay in and dwell in the first place, since he knew full well that it was inhabited by sinners before the Lord (Genesis 13:10-13), yet for the sake of personal advantage, he violated his SEPARATED stand and pitched his tent in the direction of Sodom.

b. **Lot's Failure In SEPARATION by His Contest With The Sodomites.** When God had made up His mind to destroy Sodom, and had sent the angels into the city to take out Lot and his family, the Sodomites of the city tried to seduce these angels whom they thought to be ordinary mortal men. Lot called these Sodomites "brethren" (Genesis 19:7) and then offered them his two daughters upon whom they could vent their passions (Genesis 19:8). Such action shows the failure of Lot to take a SEPARATED stand.

c. **Lot's Failure In SEPARATION By His Desire to Remain In Sodom.** As further evidence that Lot really was not in any hurry to be completely SEPARATED from unbelievers, he failed to hurry in any way as the angels tried to hasten him out of Sodom before its destruction. (Genesis 19:15-16)

3. **Esau's Failure In SEPARATION From Unbelievers.** Esau failed to exercise the duties of a SEPARATED man thus failing God, when he took unto himself a wife from the nations that were living around him rather than going back to the house of his ancestors as God would have had him and as Jacob had done previously (Genesis 26:34).

4. **Dinah's Failure In SEPARATION From Unbelievers.** Dinah, the only daughter of Jacob, failed to be too cautious in regard to her friends. She went out one day from Jacob's home to see the daughters of the land (Genesis 34:1). She was living with her father and her twelve brothers, yet she evidently had some friends among the heathen Hittites. This failure of complete SEPARATION from unbelievers in fundamental essentials occasioned her own ravaging by Shechem (Genesis 34:2).

5. **Joseph's Brethren And Their Failure In SEPARATION From Unbelievers.** Eleven of Joseph's brothers, or at least some of the eleven, were wrong enough to sell Joseph to someone else. This was a sin as it was. But to sell him to unbelieving Ishmaelites and Midianites for the sake of profit was in violation of the complete SEPARATION on their part from unbelievers in a business sense (Genesis 37:25, 27-36). The brothers were not particular who it was that bought Joseph, just so they could do away with them and get a little silver for it in return.

6. Judah's Failure in SEPARATION From Unbelievers. Judah married a Canaanite (Genesis 38:2) but this would not have been the case had he SEPARATED himself from unbelievers. As he journeyed throughout the land, away from his brethren, he turned in to an Adullamite named Hirah and there saw a Canaanite damsel who later became his wife. Judah had failed in keeping himself pure before his God by this mingling in marriage with unbelievers.

7. Jacob's Failure In SEPARATION From Unbelievers. In the time of Jacob, there was a grievous famine in the land of Canaan. Jacob, wholly without faith in the Lord who could provide for His family even in the time of famine, sent his ten sons into Egypt among the unbelievers to get food (Genesis 42:1-3; 43:3). It was clearly indicated to Isaac not to go down to Egypt and this entrance into that land seems to be out of the will of God (Genesis 26:2) even though in God's permissive will, Jacob was allowed later to journey to this land to be re-united with his long lost son, Joseph.

B. Failure In SEPARATION With Unbelievers In The Time Of Moses And The Judges.

1. Moses' Failure In SEPARATION From Unbelievers. When Moses left Egypt, he evidenced a lack of complete SEPARATION unto God by his marriage to the daughter of Reuel (Exodus 2:21), an unbeliever. There is also another instance of Moses' failure in complete devotion to the Lord in his acceptance of the advice of Jethro (a different spelling for Reuel, it is believed by some) although there is a difference of opinion on the wisdom of this advice. (Cf. Exodus 18:6 ff., 19).

2. Israel's Failure In SEPARATION From The Moabite Unbelievers. In Numbers chapter 25, the children of Israel are spoken of as committing whoredoms with the daughters of Moab. This catastrophe was not brought about by any sudden impulse, but-rather through the long time in which the Israelites had mingled themselves among the unbelieving heathen people, infiltration of ideas took place (Numbers 25:1-3) with a result that even in the realm of worship, Israel was compromised. Such activities do not indicate the SEPARATED walk of a believer, either in that time, or today.

3. Samson's Failure In SEPARATION From Unbelievers. A further character in the Bible who lived during the time of the Judges and who was not in line with God's will in the matter of SEPARATION from unbelievers, was Samson (Judges 14:1-3, 10; 16:16-17). Samson had three love affairs with unbelievers, all of which were no doubt preceded by other contacts with these heathen among whom he lived. This manner of mingling with the godless caused his downfall in the end.

4. Elimelech And Naomi's Failure In SEPARATION From Unbelievers. In the time when the Judges ruled, there was no king in Israel.

Elimelech and Naomi, his wife, left the land of blessing and promise to sojourn with unbelievers in the land of Moab (Ruth 1:1-2c, 4). They did so because of the famine that was in Bethlehem-Judah, seemingly without faith in their God to take care of them in His land. While continuing there among the unbelievers, their two sons married with the heathen--a price they had to pay for their failure.

    C. Failure In SEPARATION From Unbelievers In The Time Of The Kings.

        1. Failure In SEPARATION From Unbelievers In The United Kingdom.

            a. Saul's Failure In SEPARATION From Unbelievers. After Samuel had forsaken him, Saul, king of Israel, went to seek out a witch who lived at En-dor. The woman with a familiar spirit (1 Samuel 28:7) was at last found and though she trembled to tell him anything for fear of the king (he had disguised himself and was therefore unknown to her. She later consented to bring up Samuel. Saul seemingly had no scruples about seeking an unbelieving witch--a mark of an UNSEPARATED man.

            b. David 'a Failure In SEPARATION From Unbelievers.

                (1) David And The Philistines. David (1 Samuel 27:1, 3; 29:2, 4) violated the principles of God when he offered to go to war in the Philistine army against Israel, the people of God. The Lord defeated this attempt, however, and the Philistines prevented his going.

                (2) David and Hanun. David also tried to make friends with Hanun the Amonite after the death of his father. He wished to show kindness to this unbeliever (2 Samuel 10:1-4; 1 Kings 9:11-15; 1 Chronicles 19:1-4) and for his trouble was sorely humiliated by having the Ammonites send David's servants home half naked. This act of appeasement of an unbelieving king was out of order.

            c. Solomon's Failure In SEPARATION From Unbelievers.

                (1) Solomon And Pharaoh. Solomon made a league by marrying the daughter of the king of Egypt, an unbelieving monarch of the most pagan sort (1 Kings 3:1; 9:16). Such a league was in direct violation of the will and purpose of God, but nevertheless was permitted by the Lord.

                (2) Solomon And Hiram. As a further example of the questionable friendships that Solomon had, he bargained with Hiram who was the king of Tyre to build the holy house of the Lord (1 Kings 5:1, 5-6). Certainly Hiram was not the only king around who had the necessary cedar trees with which to build God's temple. Yet Solomon seemed to have no conscience about hiring this pagan to be his business partner.

(3) Solomon And The Queen of Sheba. So magnificent was Solomon's reign and so beautiful was the temple he had built that even the Queen of Sheba came up from Egypt to admire his kingdom (1 Kings 10:1). She tested his wisdom with difficult questions and found that his men were truly happy as she had heard. Before leaving, this pagan queen gave Solomon one hundred and twenty talents of gold worth about $19,000,000 [plus more when you include the present-day inflation] which he gladly accepted (1 Kings 10:10, 13; 2 Chronicles 9:9). With this bribe no doubt, came also some promises which Solomon felt were all right even though against the will of the Lord.

(4) Solomon And Egyptian Horses. Solomon further sinned in his walk before God by going down to Egypt in order to buy horses from these unbelievers (1 Kings 10:28-29). The Lord had forbidden any return to the land of Egypt to buy horses, but Solomon did it any way. To a man with a non-separated walk, commerce with unbelievers, in violation of God's will, it did not seem to matter.

(5) Solomon And Wives. As a crowning stroke of compromise with the unbelieving world, Solomon added to his heathen wife of Egypt no less than 1,000 more (1 Kings 11:1-9) who later on turned away his heart from the Lord to serve idols of stone and wood. This marked the sad ruin of this man who dared to toy with unbelievers.

2. Failure In SEPARATION From Unbelievers In The Divided Kingdom.

a. Abijam's Failure In SEPARATION From Unbelievers. Abijam had failed regarding SEPARATION from the matter of making a covenant with a pagan king of Syria in the form of a league (1 Kings 15:19).

b. Asa's Failure In SEPARATION From Unbelievers. Asa failed the same way as his father before him by making a league with Syria and even going so far as to give some of the treasures of his house to this unbeliever to seal the covenant (1 Kings 15:18-20; 2 Chronicles 16:2-3, 7-8).

c. Ahab's Failure In SEPARATION From Unbelievers.

(1) Ahab And Jezebel. The beginning of the downfall of Ahab, king of Israel, was when he married wicked Jezebel, whose father was Ethbaal, king of the Zidonians--an ardent worshiper of Baal. Thus, in uniting in a common purpose with this unbeliever, he failed his God (1 Kings 16:31).

(2) Ahab And Syria. This alliance with the Zidonians through marriage to Jezebel was not the last of Ahab's compromising measures with the unbelievers. He also made a league with Benhadad, the king of Syria, when the armies were surrounding Samaria (1 Kings 20:1-4, 5, 7, cf. Isaiah 7:1-4; 8:9-13). He also gave this pagan king silver, gold, and even his own wives.

d. Jehoshaphat's Failure In SEPARATION From Unbelievers.

(1) Jehoshaphat And Ahab. In direct violation and wanton disregard of God's will in making alliance with unbelievers, Jehoshaphat made a pact with wicked king Ahab (1 Kings 22:1-4, 30, 34; 2 Chronicles 18:1-3; 19:2). He even went so far in his union with this unbeliever that he said:

> *I am as thou art, my people as thy people, my horses as thy horses.*
> (1 Kings 22:4)

This indicated the sell-out to Ahab. This union was severely rebuked and broken by Hanani.

(2) Jehoshaphat And Ahaziah. As if one league with an unbeliever was not sufficient, Jehoshaphat entered into another pact, this time with king Ahaziah of Israel (2 Chronicles 20:35-37). God's Words said that Jehoshaphat joined himself to this Ahaziah king of Israel "who did very wickedly." (2 Chronicles 20:35).

e. Ahaziah's Failure In SEPARATION From Unbelievers. Ahaziah, king of Judah, the sixth king of the divided kingdom, entered into an unlawful and spiritually crippling league and pact with Jehoram, King of Israel (2 Chronicles 22:5-9). So intimate was his relation with Ahab's house that they became his counselors to do wickedly. When Jehoram, the son of Ahab, king of Israel, was sick, Ahaziah of Judah went to visit him. At this moment Jehu executed judgment on Jehoram's house and killed Ahaziah while he was there. This was the bad ending of a man who dared to compromise and fellowship with unbelievers.

f. Amaziah's Failure In SEPARATION From Unbelievers. A further example of compromise and union with unbelievers on the part of God's people is found in the case of Amaziah who hired 300,000 soldiers from the apostate kingdom of Israel to the north to fight his battles for him (2 Chronicles 25:6-10, 14-16). For these 300,000 soldiers, he had to pay one hundred talents of silver which would be about $200,000 in our currency [plus the present-day inflation on]. Rebuked for this act by a man of God, he reluctantly lost his $200,000 and sent the 300,000 soldiers back to Israel--but he won the battle with the Syrians and was blessed of God for it. His original non-separation was very unwise.

g. Uzziah's Failure In SEPARATION From Unbelievers. Uzziah of Judah was a man of whom the Scriptures said:

> *He did that which was right in the sight of the Lord, according to all that his father Amaziah did.* (2 Chronicles 26:4).

Nevertheless, his life was not without its blemishes. Because he sought God in the days of Zechariah the prophet (2 Chronicles 26:5) he could go forth to war and could defeat his enemies by God's power (1 Chronicles 26:6). Evidently the Ammonites were afraid of Uzziah and of his power which was from the Lord and they offered him gifts seemingly as a bribe (2 Chronicles 26:8). He accepted these gifts from this unbelieving nation of people and thus was not whole-hearted in his service for God.

      h.   Ahaz's Failure In SEPARATION from Unbelievers.
Ahaz, the king of Judah, was one of the wicked kings. As such, he set an example of failure in regard to SEPARATION from unbelievers. He made a league with Assyria in order to gain his help against the king of Syria whom God had sent to punish him (2 Chronicles 28:5, 16, 20-21). In his efforts to appease Assyria, he even went so far as to take a portion of the treasures of the house of the Lord and give it to Tilgathpilnezer, king of Assyria (2 Chronicles 28:20-21).

      i.   Hezekiah's Failure In SEPARATION From Unbelievers.

      (1)   Hezekiah And Egypt. Though trust in Egypt was condemned both by the prophets Isaiah and Ezekiel (Isaiah 30:1-2, 7; 31:1-3; 36:6, 9; Ezekiel 16:26), Hezekiah trusted in this heathen power in lieu of the Lord God of Israel (2 Kings 18:21) and is ridiculed about it by Rabshakeh, king of Assyria (2 Kings 18:19).

      (2)   Hezekiah and Babylon. Another failure of Hezekiah king of Judah was in the matter of Babylon. Berodachbaladan, the son of Baladan, king of Babylon, sent a present to Hezekiah because he had heard of his sickness (2 Kings 20:12). Hezekiah promptly received this present and opened his doors to receive the wicked missionaries of Babylon, even to the extent of showing them all the precious things in the house of the Lord and all the gold and silver therein. This later proved fatal (2 Kings 20:12-19; cf. Ezekiel 23:14-18).

      j.   Josiah's Failure in SEPARATION From Unbelievers.
In the time of king Josiah, king of Judah, Necho, king of Egypt came up to fight against Charchemish (2 Chronicles 35:20). King Josiah of Judah seemed to like battle because he went out against Necho, even though Necho was not intending to fight him. Despite the warnings of Necho, Josiah persisted in pursuing Necho's army and ended up by being mortally wounded by the archers (2 Chronicles 35: 21-24). Josiah had no business in battle with this pagan unbeliever who had no scruples--especially when there was no need or cause whatsoever!

    D.   Failure In SEPARATION From Unbelievers In The Time Of The Post-Exile

      1.   Ezra's People's Failure In SEPARATION From Unbelievers. After the children of Israel had returned from their captivity in

Babylon, they were still not wholly cured from sinning in the realm of mingling themselves with unbelievers who lived around about them. They persisted in making marriages with these people and not separating themselves from them (Ezra 9:1-2, 11-14). This close mingling brought about the further step of participation in these unbelievers' sins also.

2. Nehemiah's People's Failure In SEPARATION From Unbelievers.

a. Nehemiah's People's Failure In SEPARATION Regarding Marriage. As in the time of Ezra, so in Nehemiah's time, the people of Israel persisted in marrying the heathen that lived around them (Nehemiah 13:23-25). This intimate contact with unbelievers did much to corrupt the whole stock of Israel. Had not Nehemiah dealt with this problem in a clear way, the trouble would have spread much more rapidly.

b. Nehemiah's People's Failure In SEPARATION Regarding Traders. Another failure that Nehemiah's people had in connection with the unsaved unbelievers of the land was in connection with some traders (Nehemiah 13:15-22). The people of Judah were treading wine presses on the Sabbath day which was illegal according to the law of Moses. They took this merchandise and brought it into Jerusalem to the men of Tyre who were living there. They then began to sell their wares on the Sabbath day. This trading with unbelievers who had no scruples about the Sabbath day was certainly a hindrance to the spiritual progression of Israel and had to be dealt with sternly by Nehemiah. He commanded the gates to be shut during the Sabbath day and that no selling should take place on that day.

3. Esther's Failure In SEPARATION From Unbelievers. Esther is a picture of a nonseparated woman in the midst of a pagan court. Though this is not often discussed or thought about, she was not really living up to her position as a Jewess by being taken into Ahasuerus' court to be treated as a common woman as were the other virgins of Persia (Esther 2:5, 7-8, 17). It was of God's grace that Esther should be so close to the king's throne to be of use when the persecution of the Jews took place, but her marriage to this pagan, unbelieving king, under such sensual circumstances, certainly must have grieved the heart of God.

III. SUCCESS IN SEPARATION REGARDING UNBELIEVERS

A. Success In SEPARATION With Unbelievers In The Time Of The Patriarchs.

1. Enoch's Success In SEPARATION From Unbelievers. Enoch, even though not much else is said about him, "walked with God" (Genesis 5:22-24). It is said twice over that he *"walked with"* his God. So great was this man's devotion and SEPARATION unto the Lord that the Lord translated him, taking him up into the Heavens to be with Himself. He thus stood out among the antediluvians as a man of God--SEPARATED unto His Lord.

    2.   Noah's Success In SEPARATION From Unbelievers. Noah also was a man who was precious in God's sight, keeping himself unspotted from the wicked world of unbelievers who lived around him. Noah was the only one in the whole earth that was considered "just" in the sight of God (Genesis 6:8-9). Noah found "grace" in the sight of the Lord and he thus was the instrument of God in the saving of his own family and of the animals that he took with him into the ark. It would have been impossible for him to have walked with the world in an unseparated relationship, and also to have walked with his God. He chose to walk with God, and so should Christian believers today.

    3.   Abram's Success in SEPARATION From Unbelievers.

        a.   Abram And Sodom. After Lot, Abram's nephew, had been captured by the kings who took all of Sodom captive, Abram went out after these kings with only 318 trained servants to recover his relative from the clutches of the enemy. In so doing, Abram recovered the king of Sodom as well. As a payment for this deed of rescue, the king of Sodom wanted to pay Abram something. Abram, a truly SEPARATED man of God, refused this corrupt money so that the king could not say he had made Abram rich (Genesis 14:22-23).

        b.   Abram And Ephron. As further illustration from Abram's life of SEPARATION from unbelievers he refused a bargain made to him by Ephron the Hittite on the matter of a burial place (Genesis 23:3-16). Ephron suggested that Abram accept this land as a gift, but Abram would not be any man's debtor, much less an unbeliever's, and so refused the free gift, paying for it as was proper and fitting.

    4.   Jacob's Success In SEPARATION From Unbelievers.

        a.   Jacob And Laban. When Jacob went to his relative Laban's house to get his wife, he was not counting on being deceived as Laban had deceived him. He stayed a long time with Laban serving this unbeliever in a satisfactory manner. Finally he made up his mind to leave him and, even though it was against the will of Laban, made his break with this man, taking his family with him (Genesis 30:26; 31:20). It is to be noted that this marriage of Jacob was probably not so much on a religious basis (Laban's family being unbelievers), but on a racial basis, Laban being a relative and of the same stock as Abraham, Isaac, and Jacob.

        b.   Jacob And Burial. Another instance of Jacob's desiring to leave the presence of unbelievers is at his death when he made Joseph promise to bury him in the land of his fathers in Canaan instead of in the land of the heathen Egyptians (Genesis 47:30; 50:5, 11). He looked in faith to Canaan being a land of promise and blessing.

     5.   **Joseph's Success In SEPARATION From Unbelievers.** There is no better illustration of a believer's SEPARATION regarding unbelievers than in the case of Joseph. Joseph conducted himself in all godliness even though he was in the midst of perverse and wicked Egyptians who sought to tempt him and lead him into their sins (Genesis 39:1-6, 7-10 ff.). For this steadfastness, God blessed him singularly.

    B.   **Success In SEPARATION From Unbelievers In The Time Of The Kings.**

        1.   **Asa's Success In SEPARATION From Unbelievers.**

           a.   **Asa And Ethiopia.** The Ethiopian hosts numbering into the million had arrayed themselves against Asa (2 Chronicles 14:10-12). Instead of turning in weakness to the unbelievers for help, he turned to the Lord who heard and answered his prayer, bringing victory to the hosts of Judah.

           b.   **Asa and Maachah.** A further instance of Asa's SEPARATION from unbelievers concerned his own mother, queen Maachah. Asa removed her from being queen because of her idolatry and sinfulness, thus indicating his desire to remove unbelievers from prominent positions around him. (2 Chronicles 15:16).

        2.   **Jehoshaphat's Success In SEPARATION From Unbelievers.** Jehoshaphat, king of Judah was surrounded by the Ammonites who were gathered against him in Syria at Engedi. Jehoshaphat feared for his life and the life of the people, but rather than to ask help from some unholy alliance with unbelievers, he prayed unto the Lord who heard and answered with great victory over the Ammonites (2 Chronicles 20:1-4,14-18).

        3.   **Elijah's Success In SEPARATION From Unbelievers.** Elijah shows the success of a man wholly SEPARATED unto the Lord and from unbelievers when he firmly took his stand against the unbelieving prophets of Baal on mount Carmel. He asked them how long they were going to halt between two opinions (1 Kings 18:21 ff.) and ended up by dealing firmly with the unbelieving worshipers of Baal, even causing their death (1 Kings 18:40).

        4.   **Jehu's Success in SEPARATION From Unbelievers.** Jehu also dealt very firmly with pagan religion in the form of Baal worship as he came into power in Israel just after Ahab had become king (2 Kings 10:23, 25-30). Rather than to go along with this vile idolatry [although Jehu was not perfect by a long way], he followed, in this instance. at least, the will of the Lord and destroyed Baal worship from the kingdom.

        5.   **Jehoida's Success In SEPARATION From Unbelievers.** Jehoida also was firm in his stand against the pagan Baal worship that was

present in his time (2 Kings 11:18; 2 Chronicles 23:17). He both slew the priest of Baal and threw down the altars and houses of worship for this heathen god, thus making a clean sweep of this form of sin.

6. Hezekiah's Success In SEPARATION From Unbelievers. When the kingdom of Assyria was surrounding the capital of Judah, Hezekiah, the king, was in prayer before the Lord (2 Kings 19:14-19; 2 Chronicles 32:7-8; Isaiah 37:20). He did not take to heart all the vile insinuations made by Rabshakah's messengers that were aimed at belittling the God of Israel. Instead he sought help only from the Lord to go against this unbeliever.

C. Success In SEPARATION From Unbelievers In The Time Of The Exile.

1. Daniel's Success in SEPARATION From Unbelievers. Daniel remained true to his SEPARATED position before the Lord even though he was in the hands of the Babylonians, many miles away from the home of his nativity.

a. Daniel And Food. Rather than to break his rules regarding the strict Jewish diet, Daniel refused the portion of the king of Babylon's meat and the wine which he drank (Daniel 1:8, 15). Even though he went on this vegetable diet, he was still fairer than all the other captives at the end of the time of testing.

b. Daniel and Prayer. Also in the matter of prayer, Daniel walked in wholehearted trust and dependence and perseverance, even though his own life was in danger (Daniel 6:4-5, 10, 20-23). God sent His angel to shut the mouths of the lions to preserve Daniel even in their den. He walked with God even in the midst of unbelievers.

2. Shadrach, Meshach, and Abednego's Success In SEPARATION From Unbelievers.

a. Regarding Food. Just like Daniel, these three Hebrew men had refused the sinful diet offered to them by the prince of the eunuchs (Daniel 1:15) thus keeping their SEPARATION from these unbelievers' ways.

b. Regarding Idolatry. Nor did these three men bow down to the image made by king Nebuchadnezzar. They instead remained true to the Lord their God even though they were thrown into the furnace of fire (Daniel 3:11-12, 27-28). God saw them through even this test successfully.

3. Jeremiah's Success In SEPARATION From Unbelievers.

a. Jeremiah's Sitting Alone. Rather than to mingle with the unbelievers who had invaded his native country, Jeremiah "sat alone" (Jeremiah 15:17). He was a prophet who had been ordained of the Lord with a message to sinners, but he did not become entangled with these sinners in any way.

b. Jeremiah's Staying In The Land. The time came when Jeremiah was given the opportunity of choosing whether he would like to go into the land of Babylon or to stay in the land of Canaan with his countrymen and minister there. He chose the latter perhaps in accord with his desire to remain with his own people instead of the multitudes of unbelieving heathen he would find in Babylon (Cf. Jeremiah 40:4, 6).

D. Success In SEPARATION From Unbelievers In The Time Of The Post-Exile.

1. Ezra's Success In SEPARATION From Unbelievers.

a. Ezra And His Helpers. When Ezra had gone back into the land of Palestine, the heathen came to him desiring him to let them help build the wall of the city. Ezra flatly refused these heathen in their offer. He did not need their help or any other unbelievers' help in doing the work of the Lord (Ezra 4:1-5).

b. Ezra And The Soldiers. Rather than to accept soldiers from the heathen king Of Persia to accompany him on his journey, Ezra looked instead unto the Lord of Heaven and from Him received all the protection he needed (Ezra 8:22-23).

c. Ezra's People And Marriage. When the people of Ezra's time took unto themselves wives of the unbelievers round about them in the land of Canaan, Ezra called for a resolute SEPARATION from these women (Ezra 10:1-3, 11, 16). This SEPARATION was effected quickly.

2. Nehemiah's Success In SEPARATION From Unbelievers.

a. Nehemiah's People And Strangers. The people that came to Palestine with Nehemiah took their stand also to SEPARATE from the strangers of the land so that they would not marry them or have other dealings with them (Nehemiah 9:2; 10:28,,, 30).

b. Nehemiah And The Mixed Multitude. Though the mixed multitude had been with Israel as they came out of the land of Egypt, Nehemiah saw to it that these unbelievers were weeded out from the rest of Israel when they returned to the land (Nehemiah 13:3).

3. Mordecai's Success In SEPARATION From Unbelievers. Mordecai illustrated success in SEPARATION from unbelievers in a religious way by his refusal to bow before the wicked Haman, even though Haman had the power of death in his hand. So loyal was Mordecai to his God and to the commandments which forbade such a bowing to a human being that he lived a holy life (Esther 3:2).

IV. NEW TESTAMENT SEPARATION REGARDING UNBELIEVERS

A. Separation In The New And Old Testaments Compared.

1. Old And New Testament SEPARATION Compared Regarding The People Concerned. In the Old Testament, SEPARATION concerned the earthly people, Israel, with whom God had made a covenant of earthly promises. In the New Testament, SEPARATION concerns a Heavenly people, the church, whose blessings are primarily Heavenly and eternal as contrasted to earthly. The New Testament is concerned with a group of people redeemed by the blood of the Lord Jesus Christ, while the Old Testament pictures a people redeemed from Egypt by the blood of the Passover Lamb.

2. Old And New Testament SEPARATION Compared Regarding The Place. In the Old Testament, the Lord had an earthly place of one location for His people, Israel. In the New Testament, the believers are scattered throughout the whole world rather than being confined to one location. The SEPARATION from unbelievers adapted to the Old Testament covenant people of God is therefore not the same in practical outworking as the SEPARATION from unbelievers as demanded by God for His New Testament called out company, THOUGH CERTAIN PRINCIPLES ARE THE SAME.

3. Old And New Testament SEPARATION Compared Regarding God's Purpose. The purpose of God in the case of Israel and the unbelieving nations which surrounded it was the extermination and removal of the sinful people from the presence of God's own chosen race. In the New Testament, however, God's purpose is to have His chosen people, the believers constituting the church of the Lord Jesus Christ, in among the unbelievers without at the same time partaking in their sins of either flesh or spirit (2 Corinthians 7:1) and fellowshipping with them in their wicked ways.

B. SEPARATION In The Time Of The Lord Jesus Christ.

1. SEPARATION In The Time Of The Lord Jesus Christ in Regard to Christ Himself.

a. Christ And Satan. The Lord Jesus Christ was confronted early in His ministry by the Devil himself. Instead of complying to his wisdom, the Lord Jesus Christ steadfastly refused to be influenced by Satan in any way whatsoever, thus bearing up in the testing in a SEPARATED fashion to the glory of God the Father (Matthew 4:1-11).

b. Christ And The Syro-Phoenician Woman. In the life time of the Lord Jesus Christ, the law was upheld by Him. This meant that He was to go to His own people, the Jews, first of all. This He did in the case of the Syro-Phoenician woman (Mark 7:25-28) who came to Him for help.

   c. Christ And Sinners. Though the Pharisees accused the Lord Jesus Christ of receiving sinners and eating with them, He nevertheless remained holy, harmless, undefiled, and "SEPARATE from sinners" during His life on earth (Cf. Luke 7:34; 13:26; 15:1-2; Hebrews 7:26).
   d. Christ And The Samaritan Woman. In the Gospel of John, the Lord Jesus Christ dealt with the Samaritan woman, even though she was from another race--a despised race at that. This was because the Gospel of John pictured the Lord Jesus Christ, not as the king of the Jews, but as the Son of God, seeking sinners of all races of the world (John 4:4, 9).
   e. Christ and The World. The Lord Jesus Christ made it clear that He was in the world, but not of it in any real sense. This point is returned to in connection with believers of this age (John 8:23). The Lord lived a SEPARATED life even though He was surrounded by unbelievers in the world.
  2. SEPARATION In The Time Of The Lord Jesus Christ In Regard To The Twelve Apostles. At first, the twelve apostles were forbidden to go into the land of Samaria, but to go only to the Jews. After this, however, the Lord Jesus Christ told them they were to be in the presence of kings and Gentiles for His sake, thus indicating a wider sphere of witness and service (Matthew 10:5-6; Matthew 10:18). This enlarged the narrow Jewish realm of ministry tremendously.
  3. SEPARATION In The Time Of The Lord Jesus Christ In Regard To Peter. In the time of the Lord Jesus Christ, at His trial, Peter Illustrated the wrong attitude of SEPARATION from unbelievers. While His Lord was being tried in the palace, Peter was warming his hands among the unbelieving throng that had gathered to crucify Him (Mark 14:54; Luke 22:55; John 18:18). Added to this was Peter's denial three times over of His Lord. Such is NOT the norm for the believer today, by any means.
  4. SEPARATION In The Time Of The Lord Jesus Christ In Regard To The Upper Room Teaching. In the Upper Room Discourse of the Lord Jesus Christ, with His Disciples, the position of the believer of this dispensation is revealed very clearly--especially regarding the question of SEPARATION from unbelievers. The believer is said to be "in the world" but not "of the world" and therefore is to live in this present evil system as is becoming to the Lord Jesus Christ and God the Father (John 13:1; 15:18-20; 17:6, 11, 14-16, 18). For living in the world, the believer must suffer the

affliction of being persecuted by the world which does not understand him in the least because it did not understand the Lord Jesus Christ (John 15:18-20).
  C. SEPARATION In The Time Of The Book Of Acts. Throughout the book of Acts both Peter and Paul at first confined their ministries to the

Jewish people. Over and over, however, toward the end of their ministries, they went to the Gentiles also, taking the Good News of salvation by faith in the Lord Jesus Christ unto them also (Cf. Acts 9:15; 13:2, 46-48; 15:12; 18:6; 21:19; 22:21; 26:16-18; Acts 10:9-15. 45; 15:7). This reticence on the part of Peter and Paul to go to the Gentiles at first is reminiscent of Old Testament times where the Jew was to be SEPARATE from the Gentile and also in the time of the Lord's ministry where He offered Himself first to the Jews as the Messiah before turning to the Gentiles and to the world in the sense of a "whosoever will" gospel.

    D. SEPARATION In The Epistles And The Book Of Revelation.
        1. SEPARATION In The Epistles Of Paul.
            a. SEPARATION In The Book Of Romans. In Romans 12:1-2, the believer is not to defile himself with the unbelievers in the world by being conformed to their manner of life. He is rather to be transformed by the Holy Spirit who lives within him. As the believer is in the world and living among the worldlings, he is further cautioned about being "overcome of evil" (Romans 12:21). Though there is evil on every hand, the believer is to remain SEPARATE from it.

            b. SEPARATION In The Books Of 1 And 2 Corinthians.
                (1) 1 Corinthians. In 1 Corinthians 5:9-10, Paul realized that the believer cannot be entirely taken from the presence of fornicators, though he can keep himself pure from this sin. Paul gave his method of winning the Jews and the Greeks as "becoming all things to all men, that I might by all means save some" (1 Corinthians 9:22). This does NOT mean, however, that Paul compromised with sinners, yet he went in among them to win them for the Lord Jesus Christ. Nor does it mean that he joined them in joint-sponsored events with unsaved people!

                (2) 2 Corinthians. 2 Corinthians 6:14--7:1 is the classic passage on the matter of believers' SEPARATION from unbelievers, since the command is "Be ye not unequally yoked together with unbelievers . . ." This is to be taken in a multitude of senses and not to be limited only to marriage or idolatry as some have wrongly done. It has application to ecclesiological and personal SEPARATION as well in principle.

            c. SEPARATION in The Book Of Ephesians. In Ephesians 5:7, the believers are exhorted not to have fellowship or to be partakers with the unbelievers in their sins. In Ephesians 5:11, Paul wrote that Christians are to "reprove" the "unfruitful works of darkness" that are practiced by the unsaved, rather than to be in "fellowship" with them.

            d. SEPARATION In The Book Of Philippians. The place and position of the SEPARATED believer in the midst of the unbelievers is graphically pictured in Philippians 2:14-16. He is to be a "light" in the world of unbelief, going around without murmuring and complaining that he might shine forth to the wicked and perverse people with whom he comes in contact. This type of SEPARATION from unbelievers is not total withdrawal in the New Testament, as it was in the Old [although sometimes this is the only safe policy] but rather a movement among them while all the time keeping the light burning for the Lord Jesus Christ.

2. SEPARATION In the General Epistles.

a. SEPARATION In The Book Of James. In James 4:4, the friend of the world is called the "enemy of God." This is to say that the believer who loves the world more than he loves God is certainly to be sinning before the Father. The line of demarcation must always be kept rigid between the believer and the unbeliever in this day and age.

b. SEPARATION In The Book Of 1 John. In 1 John 2:15-17, the believers are cautioned "love not the world" of men nor the things that are contained in the world because of their transitory nature. This does not mean that theme should cease to be a love for the souls of the men and women, boys and girls, in the world, but it does mean that sinners should not be taken into the inner circle of friends in preference to God's own children.

c. SEPARATION In The Book Of 2 John. 2 John 10-11 makes it clear that the believer is to have no real fellowship with an apostate religionist who denies the true Christology as taught in the Bible. This could be applied readily to the modernists of today.

3. SEPARATION In The Book Of Revelation. Even in the last book of the Bible, the believer is warned through Babylon to "come out of her, my people, that ye be not partakers of her sins" (Revelation 18:4). Even Heaven itself is without sinners so why should the believer cleave to them while on the earth (Revelation 22:3-4)?

CHAPTER V
SEPARATION REGARDING DISORDERLY BELIEVERS

Dr. John R. Rice, in an issue of his newspaper, *The Sword Of The Lord*, took strong issue with regard to any sort of SEPARATION from disorderly believers. He called it "secondary separation" and said that it was not taught in the Bible. Dr. Rice is decidedly wrong and unscriptural, however, on this point, regardless of much he is correct on his teaching regarding SEPARATION from unbelievers. The two doctrines are inter-twined. In this present chapter, we will take up the following items: (1) Definition of terms; (2) separation regarding orderly believers; (3) Old Testament separation regarding disorderly believers, and (4) New Testament separation regarding disorderly believers.

I. DEFINITION OF TERMS

A. "Believers" Defined. Though the term, "believers," is a term properly used only in relation to believers in the Lord Jesus Christ in the present age of Grace, it is used in reference to Old Testament saints only by analogy. Just as the saved individual who has believed in the Lord Jesus Christ is termed a "believer," so the Israelite under the covenant relationship of the Law of Moses, could, by analogy, be termed a "believer" in the Lord his God Who had revealed Himself in a special way to His chosen people Israel. Such is the meaning of the term when used of Old Testament characters in order to keep a unity of terminology and application throughout the chapter.

B. "Orderly" Defined. A believer is termed "orderly" in the Old Testament sense of the term when he follows the Law of Moses in all of its outer demands, and most of its inner demands as well. By no means is sinless perfection to be implied by the term as it is used here. Before the law a believer could be termed an "orderly" believer who walked with God in a real way so that God was pleased with his life. Though orderly believers of the Old Testament sinned, sin was not the predominant note of their lives. An "orderly" believer in the New Testament, is one who follows to the letter and to the spirit the commands of the New Testament.

C. "Disorderly" Defined. A believer is "disorderly" in the Old Testament sense of the term when he walks in opposition to the will of God for his life, partaking of sin of various sorts, though still loosely joined to his God insofar as being a member of the covenant which God made with the race of Israel. Though some of the personages mentioned seem from all outer characteristics to be "unbelievers" their membership in the nation of Israel, as contrasted with membership in the heathen nation, gives them, by analogy, the rank of "believers" as used here, though disorderly. In the New Testament sense, "disorderly" means one who refuses to walk in accordance with New Testament teachings and apostolic commands.

D. "SEPARATION" Defined. "SEPARATION," as it is used in the Old Testament section of this chapter refers either to the practice of the orderly believer leaving the disorderly believer; the disorderly believer leaving the orderly believer; the disorderly believer being "cut off" from his people from some specific sin; or the disorderly believer being "put to death" thus being permanently "separated" from others. The following section on SEPARATION regarding orderly believers uses "SEPARATION" in the sense of selection of some believers from among other orderly believers who are to be given a special task to perform.

II. SEPARATION REGARDING ORDERLY BELIEVERS

For one reason or another God saw fit to select or SEPARATE some of His people from the vast majority of Israelites to special services. This section appears in this chapter because of its reference to "believers," though the believers are not disorderly. Among those who illustrate this principle of selectivity are: (l) Bezaleel, (2) the Nazarites, (3) the Levites, and (4) the Prophets.

A. The SEPARATION Of Orderly Believer, Bezaleel. When Moses received the orders from God to build the tabernacle which might be the gathering place of worship for all the Israelites, he needed someone to help build this place of worship so that it would be just as the Lord had commanded. Bezaleel, the son of Uri of the tribe of Judah (Exodus 31:2) was selected or SEPARATED to the task because of his wisdom, understanding, and knowledge of all manner of workmanship which God the Holy Spirit had put into his heart (Exodus 31:3). Aholiab, of the tribe of Dan, was to help Bezaleel carry out this important task of construction of the tabernacle according to the blueprint laid down by God Himself (Exodus 31:6).

B. The SEPARATION Of The Nazarites As Orderly Believers. The Nazarites were also a group of believers that had been set apart from other Israelites for a special duty in Israel.

1. The Rules For Nazarites. A Nazarite was one who first of all had SEPARATED himself **unto** the Lord (Numbers 6:2). Along with this attitude of heart, there also went the rule of SEPARATION **from** wine, strong drink, vinegar of wine, liquor of grapes, moist grapes, dried grapes, or anything made from the vine tree from the kernels to the husk (Numbers 6:3-4). His hair was also to remain long and uncut all the days of his vow, abstaining in addition, from touching any dead bodies (Numbers 6:5-9).

2. Samson The Nazarite. Samson was a Nazarite from birth, though he soon disgraced this special calling by allowing his hair to be cut off at the hands of a wicked, Philistine, heathen woman (cf. Judges 13:5, 7; 16:17-20). The part of the Nazarite vow that Samson had broken was that of complete SEPARATION **unto** the Lord. After breaking this, all the vows were but a matter of time in the matter of violation.

3. Failures of Nazarites. Other sins of the Nazarites are mentioned in Lamentations and Amos. Lamentations mentioned that, although the Nazarites were once purer than snow and whiter than milk, they had become as black as coal by comparison (Lamentations 4:7-8). Amos mentioned that the Nazarites had been given wine to drink by wicked and backsliding Israel, thus causing them to break their vows (Amos 2:11-12).

C. The SEPARATION Of The Levites As Orderly Believers. Both the regular Levites and the priests were SEPARATED from other Israelites for a special purpose.

1. The Regular Levites. By the term "regular Levites" is meant all the Levites who were not also priests. These regular Levites were SEPARATED by God and had both general and special duties.

a. The SEPARATION Of The Regular Levites. Repeatedly in Scripture, the Levites were spoken of as being a special people, set apart for God's use (Cf. Numbers 3:6, 12-13; 8:11, 13-14, 16, 41, 45, 49-51; 18:6; 2 Chronicles 23:6). They were considered by the Lord as taking the place of the firstborn, who had been spared on the eve of the departure from Egypt (Cf. Numbers 8:11, 13-14, 16) and instead of taking all the firstborn for God's service, He chose rather to take a special tribe.

b. The General Duties Of The Regular Levites. The Levites were scattered throughout the various tribes of Israel, dwelling in 48 cities, in order to keep the Law of Moses before the people, thus keeping the worship of God uppermost in the hearts of God's children. The Kohathites, the Gershonites, and the Merarites all had special duties to perform with regard to transporting the tabernacle as the Israelites moved from place to place in their wilderness wanderings (Numbers 4:1-33).

c. The Special Duties Of The Regular Levites. For special duties, the Levites were divided into various courses (1 Chronicles 23:1-32); they were grouped into 24 orders of singers (1 Chronicles 25:1-31); they were made porters (1 Chronicles 26:1-28); and others were appointed as officers and judges (1 Chronicles 26:29-32).

2. The Priests. From the Levites, God chose the family of Aaron to be given the special distinction of priests, Aaron himself being the High Priest.

a. The Priestly Family Of Aaron. Aaron was appointed as the priestly head of Israel at an early time, though this fact was questioned by Korah and his band of rebels.

(1) Korah's Rebellion. While Israel was in the wilderness, Korah, a Levite, along with some of the other Levites, came to Moses and told him that he was taking too much upon himself in the way of responsibility. Korah, the spokesman, wondered why all the congregation could not function as Moses and Aaron (Numbers 16:1-3). Korah was to get his band together with censors and come before the presence of the Lord (Numbers 16:6-7) and God would then make manifest whom He had chosen as priests. The fire of the Lord consumed a total of 250 men that offered incense (Numbers 16:35) as a proof that these were not to be priests.

(2) Aaron's Family Set Apart. By the budding of Aaron's rod in a distinct sense, God set Aaron's family apart for priestly service once and for all (Numbers 17:1-13). The Scriptures refer many times to the family of Aaron as being the priestly family and as such, distinct from other Levites (Cf. Exodus 28:1, 3-4, 41; 29:1, 4, 9, 44; 30:30; 40:15; Numbers 3:3, 9-10; 18:1-7; 1 Chronicles 24:1 ff.; 2 Chronicles 23:6).

b. The High Priest. The high priest was set apart as different from either the general Levites or the priests. It was his job to do special things that were forbidden both the Levites and the priests.

(1) Aaron As High Priest. Inasmuch as Aaron was with Moses his brother from the beginning of Israel's redemption from Egypt, he was no doubt selected by God from all the priests and Levites to be the first high priest. As such, he was the only one who could go into the tabernacle during the day of Atonement (Numbers 16:2 ff.) which was one of the seven annual feasts of Israel. On this one day in the year, he represented the whole nation of Israel before the Lord in a special way, offering first for his own sins and then for the sins of Israel and thus gaining access to the very Holy of Holies through the shedding of blood (Leviticus 16:3, 5-6, 11, 15).

(2) Aaron's Successors. Because of Aaron's sin in rebelling against the Lord at the water of Meribah (Numbers 20:24), he was not to enter the land, but was told of God to ascend Mount Hor and to die there (Numbers 20:25). Aaron was to be stripped of his high priestly garments which were than to be given to his son, Eleazar, who was to be the next high priest (Numbers 20:25-28). Thus a new high priest was selected from the immediate family upon the death of the former high priest from that time forth.

D. The SEPARATION Of The Prophets As Orderly Believers. The prophets were another group of individual believers in Israel who were called out of their occupations to serve the Lord God of Israel in a special way.

1. The Purpose Of The Prophets. The purpose of the prophets both expressed and illustrated is essential to an understanding of this special class of believers in the Old Testament age.

a. The Purpose Of The Prophets Expressed. The prophets were definitely connected with disorderly believers in the realm of the Israelites. They were to go to such disorderly people and attempt to restore them to a place of fellowship once more with the God whom they had sinned against. They would correspond to the preachers of today, except the prophets had a more authoritative message inasmuch as it was fresh from the Lord Himself in a real way.

b. The Purpose Of The Prophets Illustrated.

(1) Ahijah, Jehu, and Eliab As Prophets. Ahijah the Shilonite was sent by God to warn disorderly king Jeroboam of the impending rebellion of 10 of the tribes of Israel because of his sins (1 Kings 11:29 ff.). Jehu the prophet was sent to king Baasha of Israel, a man whose disorderly sinful habits was to bring judgment upon his entire household. Jehu was to warn Baasha of the impending doom upon his family (1 Kings 16:7, 12). Elijah the prophet warned all Israel and Ahab because of their disorderliness (1 Kings 18:22; 19:14); he sent a letter of condemnation to Jehoram, king of Judah, in order to restore him to God (2 Chronicles 21:12); and in the latter days Elijah will return to a place of prominence among Israel as he tries to "turn the heart of the fathers to the children, and the heart of the children to their fathers . . ." (Malachi 4:5-6).

(2) Shemiah, Zechariah, and Obed As Prophets. The prophet Shemiah was sent to disorderly Rehoboam because of his wickedness (2 Chronicles 12:5 ff.). Zechariah the son of Jehoida the priest, warned Joash against transgressing the commandments of the Lord (2 Chronicles 24:20). Obed the prophet went out to Samaria to proclaim God's message to wicked king Ahaz (2 Chronicles 28:9 ff.).

(3) Urijah, Jeremiah, ant Haggai As Prophets. The prophet Urijah was sent to Jehoiakim (Jeremiah 26:20). Jeremiah himself warned disorderly Zedekiah (2 Chronicles 36:12). Haggai was sent to minister to the returned exiles of Israel and Judah who returned after their captivities to Jerusalem (Ezra 5:1-2; 6:14).

(4) All The Other Prophets. In various portions of the Old Testament, various unnamed prophets are said to have come to disorderly Israel at different times, speaking unto them the Words of God in an attempt to restore them to God's favor (Cf. 2 Kings 17:13; 21:10-12; 24:2; 2 Chronicles

24:19; 36:16; Ezra 9:11; Nehemiah 9:26, 30; Jeremiah 7:25; 25:4; 26:5; 29:19; 35:15; 44:4; Daniel 9:10; Hosea 12:10; Zechariah 1:4).

2. The Reception Of The Prophets. The reception of the prophets of God by the people was not always favorable, in fact seldom was it true.

a. The Prophetic Message Unheeded. Though God faithfully sent His servants the prophets to disorderly and sinful Israel and Judah, they would not listen to the message and repent of their sins, and turn to the Lord (Cf. Nehemiah 9:30; Jeremiah 25:4; 26:5; 29:19; 35:15; Daniel 9:10; Zechariah 1:4).

b. Some Prophets Were Punished. Jeremiah faced his disorderly crowd with fearlessness as they threatened to "smite him with the tongue" (Jeremiah 18:18) by way of verbal reproach. They later put him in stocks because he dared to tell them the truth.

c. Some Prophets Were Killed. Still other of the prophets sent by God to Israel and Judah were killed for telling these people of God's truth (cf. 1 Kings 18:13; 19:1, 10, 14; 2 Kings 9:7; Nehemiah 9:26; Lamentations 2:20; Jeremiah 2:30; Jeremiah 26:8). Had those prophets compromised the Words of God, they would probably not suffered unto death. Their death was a tribute to their faithfulness and SEPARATED stand unto their God.

3. The Failures Of The Prophets. Not all the prophets mentioned in the Words of Got did their job assigned to them. Some failed to carry out their commission to preach God's truth to His people as His SEPARATED prophets. These failed to warn the disorderly of the people to return to God. They failed in their personal life, in their preaching, and in their results. They were COMPROMISERS--not SEPARATED unto the Lord.

a. Failures Of Some Prophets In Their Personal Life. Twelve things stood out in the personal lives of the disobedient, non-separated prophets of Israel and Judah:

(1) **They were drunken** (Isaiah 28:7).
(2) **They were asleep** (Isaiah 29:10).
(3) **They were ashamed** (Jeremiah 2:26).
(4) **They were covetous** (Jeremiah 6:13; 8:10).
(5) **They dealt falsely** (Jeremiah 6:13; 8:10).
(6) **They were wicked** (Jeremiah 23:11, 15).
(7) **They were adulterous** (Jeremiah 23:14).
(8) **They were liars** (Jeremiah 23:14; Micah 2:11).
(9) **They were light** (Jeremiah 23:32; Zephaniah 3:4).
(10) **They were out for money** (Ezekiel 22:25; Micah 3:11).
(11) **They were fools** (Hosea 9:7).

(12) **They were as bad as Sodom and Gomorrah** (Jeremiah 23:14). This is a dark picture of God's men who were supposed to sound the alarm against sin and wrong doing to His people, but went from SEPARATION to COMPROMISE to APOSTASY.

  b. Failures Of Some Prophets In Their Preaching. The disobedience of the sinful, COMPROMISING prophets in their personal life had an effect in their preaching as well.

  (1) **They taught lies** (Isaiah 9:15; Jeremiah 23:25-26, 32).
  (2) **They prophesied by Baal** (Jeremiah 2:8; 23:13).
  (3) **They prophesied falsely** (Jeremiah 5:31).
  (4) **They strengthened the hand of evildoers** (Jeremiah 23:14).
  (5) **They were without God's message** (Jeremiah 23:21-22; Lamentations 2:9, Ezekiel 13:2).

  c. Failures of Some Prophets In Their Results. Certainly prophets who erred in personal life and failed to preach the true message of God through their COMPROMISE and NON-SEPARATED life, could not have failed to have been a poor example in their poor effect on the people of Israel who listened to them. The effects of such COMPROMISE on their part were all evil:

  (1) **They did not cause Israel to hear the Words of God** (Jeremiah 23:22)
  (2) **They were without profit to God's people** (Jeremiah 23:32).
  (3) **They caused Israel to err** (Jeremiah 23:13, 32; Micah 3:5).

III. OLD TESTAMENT SEPARATION REGARDING DISORDERLY BELIEVERS

This section begins the most vital part of the present Chapter, since it begins the discussion of disorderly believers in the Old Testament times. SEPARATION in the Old Testament times was of two sorts: SEPARATION by leaving, and SEPARATION by death. The SEPARATION by death is often overlooked in this consideration of the subject of BIBLICAL SEPARATION.

  A. Old Testament SEPARATION Regarding Disorderly Believers By Leaving. When a disorderly believer and an orderly believer were at variance, either the disorderly person left the orderly one, or the orderly left the disorderly, depending on the circumstances. This seemed to be God's way of dealing with the problem. For Dr. John R. Rice to have stated in the *Sword of the Lord* that the Bible did not teach that orderly believers were to SEPARATE themselves from disorderly believers is to have admitted gross Biblical ignorance, since it is SO very CLEARLY taught in the Words of God in the Old Testament as well as the New Testament. At this point, at least, Dr. Rice cannot be followed as a present-day Biblical leader. In fact, this type of rationalization away of the Bible is at the very root of COMPROMISE which is at the root of all NEW-EVANGELICALISM and the justification of the false position of the NATIONAL ASSOCIATION OF EVANGELICALS (N.A.E.) and of the BILLY GRAHAM EVANGELISTIC ASSOCIATION (B.G.E.A.).

1. **SEPARATION By The Disorderly Leaving The Orderly.**

  a. **Disorderly Cain Leaving Orderly Adam and Eve.** After Cain had committed the first murder in the history of the race of man, God cursed the ground on his account (Genesis 4:11-12) and told Cain that he would be a fugitive and a vagabond on the earth, thus driving him out from the association with Adam and Eve, his parents (Genesis 4:12, 14). This was God's method of dealing with the disorderliness of Cain. Cain may be considered on the analogy of a believer inasmuch as he was a son of Adam and Eve. The question of Cain's salvation in reality, however, is another issue.

  b. **Disorderly Lot Leaving Orderly Abram.** When Abram and Lot went up out of Egypt together after Abram's denial of Sarai as his wife, they were both in the possession of many flocks. So great was their difficulty with the flocks that Lot SEPARATED himself from Abram and departed to dwell in the land of Sodom and Gomorrah--wicked, sinful cities (Genesis 13:5-14).

  c. **Disorderly Hagar Leaving Orderly Abram And Sarai.** Hagar could be considered a "believer" in the sense that she was one of the members of Abram's household. As such, she afforded illustration of how a disorderly believer SEPARATES herself from orderly believers such as Abram and Sarah. Seeing the Egyptian's son making a mockery of Isaac, Sarah said:
  Cast out this bondwoman and her son: for the son of this bondwoman shall not be heir with my son, even with Isaac. (Genesis 21:9-10).

  d. **Disorderly Lepers Leaving Orderly Israel.** Believers of the Israelites were to be SEPARATED from their fellow believers if they were lepers, and this could be considered a type of "disorderliness" on account of the sickness. If the plague of leprosy was of a certain sort, the person was to be shut up for seven days, away from the rest of the congregation (Leviticus 13:5 ff.).

  e. **Disorderly Manslayers Leaving Orderly Israel.** If an Israelite killed another Israelite, that disorderly person was to flee to one of the six cities of refuge until the death of the High Priest, whether he was guilty of murder or mere manslaughter (Numbers 35:11, 13, 32).

  f. **Disorderly Unclean Persons Leaving Orderly Clean Israelites.** During the march of the Israelites from Egypt to the land of Canaan, by way of the wilderness, an unclean person was not to be mixed in with other of the Israelites, but was to be kept outside the camp until such a time as he could wash himself with water and thus be cleansed (Deuteronomy 23: 10-11).

2. SEPARATION By The Orderly Leaving The Disorderly. On other occasions, the orderly believers leave the presence of the disorderly and thus effect a SEPARATION from the disorderly believers. Such was the case with the following.

a. Orderly Abram Leaving Disorderly Lot. While it is true that Lot left Abram in Genesis 13, it is also true that first of all Abraham SEPARATED himself from Lot. It was Abram who first suggested the SEPARATION of Lot from him. By Lot's removal, Abram also became SEPARATED (cf. Genesis 13:8, 12, 14). He did not want dissension in the ranks and thus asked Lot to leave. It was only after this that God spoke to Abraham.

b. Orderly Jacob Leaving Disorderly Esau. After Jacob had succeeded in cheating Esau out of his blessing from Isaac, Jacob removed himself from Esau fearing his wrath (Genesis 27:41-45; cf. Genesis 32:3-4 ff.; 33:4, 9). Jacob also SEPARATED himself from disorderly Laban who had changed his wages ten times after first deceiving him on his wedding night by giving him Leah instead of Rachel (Genesis 30:25; 31:17).

c. Orderly Joseph Leaving Disorderly Brothers. Though it was not willingly, still Joseph left his wicked brothers and was sold by them into the slavery of the Egyptians. Later on he was to become the salvation of all the family of Israel by providing grain for Jacob and his sons and grandsons during the time of famine. Joseph was therefore reconciled to his once disorderly brothers (Cf. Genesis 37:18, 27; 42:3-9 ff; 45.1-8).

d. Orderly Levites Leaving Disorderly Israelites. Just after Moses had received the Law from the hand of God (Exodus 20-31), Aaron followed the pleading of the people and made a golden calf for the Israelites to worship. When Moses heard from Mount Sinai the commotion, that was made in the camp, he was filled with anger and came down from the Mount. The Levites were ordered to SEPARATE themselves from the sinning throng to slay the guilty (Exodus 32:1-6, 20-28). 3,000 men were killed in this way.

e. Orderly Moses and Aaron Leaving Disorderly Israel. In the time of the rebellion of Korah, Moses and Aaron were ordered SEPARATED by God from the sinning throng so that the guilty court be slain as well as all of the Israelites. God was going to make of Moses and Aaron a new people evidently, but repented of that thought after Moses' prayer (Numbers 16:21 ff.).

f. Orderly Moses And The Judges Of Israel Leaving Disorderly Israelites. After Balaam's prophecies for Balak the king of Moab, Israel turned to whoredom and union with the heathen practices of Baal-peor

(Numbers 25:1-3). Moses and the judges of Israel were commanded by God to come out from that multitude of sinful and DISORDERLY Israelites who should have known better. Moses was to slay every guilty person, making a total of 24,000 who died altogether (Numbers 25:4-9).

      g. Orderly David Leaving Disorderly Saul. When Saul became envious of David and hateful of this man who had done so much for Israel, David fled from his presence (1 Samuel 23:13). This was thought the best plan by Jonathan and David as well, since Saul's mind was made up to slay David.

      h. Orderly Israel's Leaving Disorderly Rehoboam. After the sins and excesses of Solomon, king of both Judah and Israel, Rehoboam took over his father's throne. Rehoboam could have listened to the old men's counsel which was of God, but he chose to listen to the counsel of the young men who had grown up with him. This fact proved to the 10 tribes that Rehoboam would continue in the sins of his father so they left the kingdom (1 Kings 12:16-19). They too were soon to fall into sin, however.

    B. Old Testament SEPARATION Regarding Disorderly Believers By Death. Not only was there a SEPARATION of the disorderly believer by leaving, but there was also (in the dispensation of the Law of Moses) various sins and evils for which death to the violator was assigned. Sometimes this death is spoken of as a "cutting off" while at other times it is spoken of as a "death" in clear term.

      1. SEPARATION by The Disorderly Being "Cut Off." Though there has been much speculation as to the meaning of the phrase "cut off," it seems that it has reference to death, or a punishment that is just as bad when compared to offenses which called for "death" in plain language. It might also mean a sort of "disfellowshipping" however.

      a. SEPARATION Of The Disorderly by Being Cut Off Regarding Circumcision. The fact that a man had not been circumcised was grounds enough for his being cut off from his people, since he had broken the covenant of circumcision (Genesis 17:14). This is one offence which was punishable by the SEPARATION of the disorderly by death.

      b. SEPARATION of the Disorderly By Being Cut Off Regarding Leaven. If during the time of the exodus from Egypt there was any leaven found in any of the houses of the Israelites, that person who owned the house was to be cut off from his people (Exodus 12:15, 19).

      c. SEPARATION Of The Disorderly By Being Cut Off Regarding Incense. When the tabernacle was set up, a perfumed incense was compounded after a certain formula. If there was any copying of this specific formula, that person would be cut off from his people, whether he was a stranger or an Israelite (Exodus 30:33).

d. SEPARATION of the Disorderly By Being Cut Off Regarding The Sabbath. The Sabbath day was to be kept as a holy day by all Israelites. If there was anyone among the children of Israel who failed to sanctify this day as a day of absolute rest, doing any work therein, that soul should be cut off from his people by death (Exodus 31:14; cf. 31:14-15; 35:2; Numbers 15:35-36).

e. SEPARATION of the Disorderly By Being Cut Off Regarding The Peace Offerings. The peace offering was not to be eaten by an unclean priest. If this were done, the priest offending in this regard was to be cut off from his people (Leviticus 7:20). The same was true if the peace offering was not completely eaten by the third day (Leviticus 19:8).

f. SEPARATION of the Disorderly by Being Cut Off Regarding Fat. So precious was the fat of the offerings in the sight of God that no one was to eat any of the fat for themselves. It was to be burned on the altar before the Lord as representing the best part of the animal. If a priest or any other person was to eat the fat of an ox, of a sheep, or of a goat, he was to be cut off from his people (Leviticus 7:23-25).

g. SEPARATION of the Disorderly By Being Cut Off Regarding Blood. Another offence which was considered by God to have been a serious crime and hence punishable by being cut off was the sin of eating the blood of any kind (Leviticus 7:27; 17:10, 14). It was the life of all flesh and one day it was to be used as the redemptive power for sinners who believe in the Lord Jesus Christ. To eat the blood which was to be a symbol of salvation and eternal life was to desecrate it.

h. SEPARATION of the Disorderly by Being Cut Off Regarding Offerings. If a person would slay an animal and then offer it on an altar outside the camp of Israel during their wanderings instead of bringing it into the tabernacle, this person was to be cut off from his people (Leviticus 17:4, 9). Though God is everywhere, nevertheless He desired His chosen people, Israel, to offer only in the proper place rather than to offer as did the heathen under every green tree.

I. SEPARATION of the Disorderly By Being Cut Off Regarding Sexual Offences. The offender in any sexual way that had been mentioned in Leviticus 18:6-23, was considered being guilty of a sin worthy of death, though in this chapter it is spoken of as a sin worthy of being "cut off" from the people for this disorder. All sorts of sexual sins are enumerated (Cf. Leviticus 18:6-23; 18:29; 19:20; 20:17-18). Believers who walked in these sins were thus punished.

j. SEPARATION of the Disorderly By Being Cut Off Regarding Molech. The Israelites were troubled during their journey in the wilderness by various heathen nations and their worship of idols. One of the their wicked practices was connected with the worship of Molech, where children were actually sacrificed by fire unto this idol. These practices of the worship of Molech on the part of any of God's children was expressly forbidden by the Lord and given a sentence of being cut off from the people for anyone who violated God's will in this matter (Leviticus 20:3, 5).

k   SEPARATION Of the Disorderly by Being Cut Off Regarding Wizards. Another sin for which the Israelites were given the penalty of being cut off from their people was the sin of turning for consultation to wizards or any who had familiar spirits (Leviticus 20:6). Evidently this practice was used in Israel's day much as spiritism is practiced in the present time. All such disorderly persons were separated from Israel.

l.   SEPARATION of the Disorderly By Being Cut Off Regarding The Day Of Atonement. One of the seven religious feasts of Israel was the feast of atonement in which every soul was supposed to afflict himself in some way or other. Any person who failed to carry out this measure of self-affliction was to be cut off from his people (Leviticus 23:29).

m.   SEPARATION of the Disorderly By Being Cut Off Regarding The Passover. The feast of Passover was another of the seven Jewish yearly feast days that had been set apart by God. As the Israelites journeyed in the wilderness, they had forgotten to observe the Passover on the proper dray (the 14th day of the first month, cf. Leviticus 23:5). Instead of observing it on the first month, the Lord asked Moses to commemorate it on the second month on the 14th day of the month (Numbers 9:9-11). If anyone failed to keep this Passover, whether clean or unclean, he was to be cut off from his people, so grave was this offence (Numbers 9:10-13).

n.   SEPARATION of the Disorderly By Being Cut Off Regarding Sinning. After discussing the sins of ignorance which it was possible for an Israelite to commit, Moses mentioned the presumptuous sin of willfulness. To thus sin in full knowledge of the truth of God's will was a disgrace and a reproach to the Lord and consequently was to be punished by the person's being cut off from his people (Numbers 15:30-31).

o.   SEPARATION of the Disorderly By Being Cut Off Regarding Purification. The touching of a dead body was enough to make an Israelite ceremonially unclean. If such a person would not avail himself of the means of purification before he entered the tabernacle, he was to be cut off from his people (Numbers 19:13,20). He should have used the water of SEPARATION (Numbers 19:13).

2.   SEPARATION By The Disorderly Being Put To Death. This separation is a permanent one, by means of death. It is most clear, however, that this was to be one means in the Old Testament time of SEPARATING the disorderly believers from those who were ORDERLY.

BIBLICAL SEPARATION By Pastor D. A. Waite, Th.D., Ph.D. **73**

a. SEPARATION of the Disorderly By Death Regarding Sinai. At Mount Sinai when Moses received the Law from the hand of God, no Israelite other than the ones designated by Moses and God to accompany Moses on his journey up the mountain was to touch Sinai. If a person did touch the mountain, he would be immediately punished by death. This referred as much to beasts as it did to man (Exodus 19:12-13).

b. SEPARATION of the Disorderly By Death Regarding Murder. Though there was room for question in certain cases of homicide, the case of murder was always punishable by death under the statutes of the Mosaic Law (Cf. Exodus 21:12, 15; Leviticus 24:17, 21; Numbers 35:16-18, 21, 30-31; Deuteronomy 19:11-13). This death was to be accomplished by lawful and orderly means, however, rather than being something rashly executed.

c. SEPARATION of the Disorderly By Death Regarding Kidnaping. Another sin for which the sentence of death was prescribed in the Old Testament is that of kidnaping (Exodus 21:16). The Israelites were not to sell their fellow human beings to others as merchandise as the heathen made a practice of doing,

d. SEPARATION of the Disorderly by Death Regarding Cursing, The son of any Israelite was expressly forbidden to curse his mother or father. Such disrespect was to be punished by the child's death (Exodus 21:17; Leviticus 20:9). Similarly they were to punish a son who cursed or blasphemed the Lord (Leviticus 24:14, 16, 23).

e. SEPARATION of the Disorderly By Death Regarding Oxen. If an ox were to gore a man or a woman so that the person died, the ox was to be stoned. If the owner was fully aware of this ox's tendencies to kill men and women, however, and did not take the precautions of keeping him in check by some means, and the ox killed a man--both the ox and the man who owned him were to be SEPARATED by death from the congregation (Exodus 21:28-29).

f. SEPARATION of the Disorderly by Death Regarding The Sabbath. The seventh day was to be called the Lord's Sabbath and no work of any sort was to be done on that day other than the necessary duties of life. If anyone were to violate this day and work therein, he was to be killed (Exodus 31:14-15; 35:2). As illustration of the severity with which this law was carried out, the Bible mentions that case of a man being put to death for gathering sticks on the Sabbath day (Numbers 15:35-36).

g. SEPARATION of the Disorderly By Death Regarding Molech. As a proof that the phrase "cut off" had to do with the death penalty, Leviticus 20:2-5 mentions in the same context both the penalty of "cutting off" and the penalty of "death" for the sin of offering any of the children of Israel by fire to the idol Molech (Leviticus 20:2, 5). Though this is not conclusive proof, it, together with other similar uses of the two penalties for the same offense tends to prove the equality of these two punishments.

h. SEPARATION of the Disorderly by Death Regarding Wizards. The consultation of wizards or those who were possessed of the evil spirits was certainly a serious crime. Those who had familiar spirits or who were wizards in any sense of this term were to be put to death, whether they were men or women (Leviticus 20:27). This crime was also punishable by the offender's being "cut off."

i. SEPARATION of the Disorderly by Death Regarding Sexual Offenses. The sins of sexual excess are given in later accounts in the Law as being not only punishable by "cutting off" but also in plain language by being put to death. This also proves the identity of these two terms since it would not be natural to have two penalties for the same offense in Scripture, thus setting up a contradiction. The sins included in the list of those punishable by death are: (1) Adultery (Leviticus 20:10; cf. John 8:4-5); (2) incest (Leviticus 20:11); (3) homosexuality (Leviticus 20:13); (4) male contact with beasts (Leviticus 20:15); (5) female contact with beasts (Leviticus 20:16); (6) prostitution (Deuteronomy 22:21); and (7) fornication with a virgin betrothed unto a husband (Deuteronomy 22:23-25).

j. SEPARATION of the Disorderly By Death Regarding The Tabernacle. Since the tabernacle in the wilderness was mobile and had to be carried from place to place by the Levites, there was a possibility for a non-Levite to attempt to help out in this transportation venture. Such an attempt was to be punished by death (Numbers 1:51). In a similar manner, the non-priests were not to attempt to work into the functions that had already been assigned to the priests of the Lord. If a stranger were to commit this sin and thus enter the sanctuary of the Lord which was only the prerogative of a priest, that stranger was to be put to death for defiling of God's tabernacle (Numbers 3:10, 38; 16:29; 18:7).

k. SEPARATION of the Disorderly by Death Regarding False Prophets. So jealous was God to keep His people pure and free from every taint of sin that He stipulated the death penalty for every prophet that taught Israel to depart from the Lord their God by preaching in favor of idolatry or similar things (Deuteronomy 13:5, 9-10). The same punishment was reserved for the prophet who added to God's message in any way (Deuteronomy 18:20).

l. SEPARATION of the Disorderly By Death Regarding Idolatry. The first commandment that God gave to Moses (Exodus 20) was in regard to idolatry. God did not want His people to set up any idols or images that would thus be used as objects of worship. The punishment for this sin and disorderly conduct was death (Deuteronomy 17:5-7). Had this penalty been observed with more diligence, there would not have been so much idolatry rampant in Israel as there was.

m. SEPARATION of the Disorderly By Death Regarding Disobedient Sons. The family relationship was one that was of extreme interest to God. The children were to remain in obedience to their parents until a certain age. This was no doubt to teach them obedience to the Lord as they later would find need. In one case there was a child who was stubborn and rebellious and who wouldn't hear his parents in obedience. This son was to be taken before the elders of the city and then taken out to be stoned by the men of the city, thus being put to death for his obedience (Deuteronomy 21:18-21).

n. SEPARATION of the Disorderly by Death Regarding Disobedience To Joshua. Joshua was put in the place of Moses who had sinned and was thus forbidden to enter the land of Canaan. Joshua was not just to be a figure-head, but was to be obeyed in the same manner as was Moses. Any disobedience to Joshua was to be punishable by death (Joshua 1:18).

o. SEPARATION of the Disorderly by Death Regarding Spoil. The reason for Israel's failure to capture Ai on the first try was the sin of Achan who had taken as a spoil a goodly Babylonish garment and about $490.00 worth of silver and $490.00 worth of gold. This was in direct disobedience to the command of Joshua and the will of God (cf. Joshua 7:11, 20-21, 25). It was therefore punished by death.

p. SEPARATION of the Disorderly by Death Regarding Belial. In the latter part of the book of Judges (cf. Judges 20), Israel had mixed themselves with the children of Belial. Most of the offenders were of the tribe of Benjamin rather than being from all the tribes (Judges 20:12-13). When the other tribes heard about how the Levite had cut up his wife into pieces and how others of the tribe of Benjamin had committed lewdness and folly in Israel (Judges 20:5-6), they came to the tribe of Benjamin and demanded that the men who had thus committed the sin of mixing with these children of Belial should be put to death (Judges 20: 13). The men of Benjamin refused to yield up these men and so a battle followed.

q. SEPARATION of the Disorderly by Death Regarding Mispah. In the same situation in the book of Judges (21:5) all Israelites who did not come up to the Lord unto Mizpah should have been put to death. This meeting in Mizpah was of such importance, evidently that the death penalty was assigned to violators.

r. SEPARATION of the Disorderly by Death Regarding Shimei. Shimei was one of the men who crossed king David's path during his many travels. He showed great lack of respect for the king by cursing him and railing at him. At first David did not want Shimei put to death for cursing him (2 Samuel 19:21), but later on, in the reign of Solomon, David's son, Shimei was sentenced to death for his wicked sin of cursing the Lord's anointed, thus being SEPARATED for his disorderliness (1 Kings 2:8-9, 36-46).

      s. **SEPARATION of the Disorderly by Death Regarding Seeking The Lord.** As another illustration of the separation of the disorderly of Israel by a penalty of death, the event in the life of King Asa must be brought up. During one part of his life, king Asa and the people entered into a solemn covenant with the Lord (2 Chronicles 15:12). The penalty of death was assigned to all those who failed to enter into this covenant with Asa and the rest of the people to seek the Lord God of Israel (2 Chronicles 15:13).

      t. **SEPARATION of the Disorderly by Death Regarding Adonijah.** Adonijah was one of David's sons, though not the one who was picked to be the next king of Israel and Judah. For his rebellion against Solomon, he was given the sentence of death (1 Kings 2:24). The sentence was executed by Benaiah the son of Jehoida (1 Kings 2:25).

IV. NEW TESTAMENT SEPARATION REGARDING DISORDERLY BELIEVERS

      Having discussed the various reasons in the Old Testament for SEPARATION from disorderly believers of the nation of Israel, there remains for this section the consideration of the New Testament cases of SEPARATION regarding disorderly believers. A definition of terms similar to that made for the Old Testament part of the study is in order before the passages are taken up.

      A. **Definition of Terms.** In the Old Testament study of the previous section, there was more of a need for a definition of terms. Even in this New Testament part, a similar definition would clarify the subject greatly.

      1. **"Believers."** The usual definition of a "believer" will be used in this New Testament part of the study. A "believer" is one who has exercised personal, saving faith in the Lord Jesus Christ as his personal sin bearer and Savior. This believer may not have been saved for a very long time, but if he or she has been justified by faith in the sight of God, the name of "believer" or "Christian" applies.

      2. **"Orderly."** An "orderly" believer is one who is walking in the light as God is in the light, confessing all known sin (1 John 1:9) and trying by every way possible in the revealed Words of God to let his light so shine before men that they may glorify their Father which is in Heaven. An "orderly" believer is not necessarily or even actually sinlessly perfect, for this is not possible in this present life. He is merely one who tries to let the fruit of the Spirit be manifested through his life moment by moment.

      3. **Disorderly."** Any believer who sins or who lives in sin for certain lengths of time is a "disorderly" believer, though not all the sins mentioned in the New Testament are of sufficient gravity for that "disorderly" believer to be SEPARATED from other believers. Every believer at one time or another is "disorderly" throughout the years of his life on earth, but for those who have submitted to certain definite sins that have been mentioned in Paul's writings, there is special note to be taken.

4. "SEPARATION." As contrasted to the SEPARATION called for in the Old Testament in the case of "disorderly" believers, in the New Testament, there is no thought of death for the disorderly; no matter how grave his sin has been. Only that type of SEPARATION which pertains to the believers withdrawing their fellowship and privileges of worship to that individual is thought of in the New Testament sense of SEPARATION as it pertains to disorderly brethren. Much controversy rages over the method of SEPARATION and the subjects of SEPARATION in this case, but the present-day application of these Pauline doctrines will be left to the individual who might wish to pursue ecclesiastical SEPARATION more in detail.

B. Passages On New Testament SEPARATION From Disorderly Believers.

1. New Testament SEPARATION Passages From Disorderly Believers That Are Disputed.

a. 1 Timothy 6:1-5. In 1 Timothy, Chapter 6, verses 1-5, Paul mentioned briefly the relationship of servants to their masters (6:1-20. The servants are to count their masters as worthy of all honor so that the name of the Lord is not blasphemed. If any one does not teach and exhort such things (6:2c), and does not consent to such wholesome words and to godly doctrine, Paul said that he is proud and knowing nothing (1 Timothy 6:4). It is entirely conceivable that the man who would teach those things would be a believer in the Lord Jesus Christ, but perhaps had not given as diligent obedience as he should have had to the doctrinal side of his Christian ministry. Paul told Timothy to "withdraw" or SEPARATE himself from such. It is recognized that the words translated "from such WITHDRAW thyself" (1 Timothy 6:5b) are not in all of the Greek texts, but since they are in the Received Text, I believe them to be genuine [see my book, *DEFENDING THE KING JAMES BIBLE*, ($12.00 plus P & H). Order from THE BIBLE FOR TODAY, 900 Park Avenue, Collingswood, N.J. 08108. It gives an in-depth discussion on this point.] If indeed the words are to be retained and if the reference is conceivably to believers who are teaching false doctrine, then it illustrates SEPARATION from disorderly believers.

b. 2 Timothy 2:20-21. A second doubtful passage pertaining to SEPARATION from disorderly believers is found in 2 Timothy 2:20-21 where Paul made mention of a great house (2:20). Though it is held by some that the great house is professing Christendom composed of both saved and lost, it is entirely possible that the "great house" might instead refer to the house of true believers, some carnal and similar to wood and earth, others spiritual and similar to gold and silver. This analogy goes in the same channel as the one used by Paul in 1 Corinthians 3:9-15.

If believers are to be in mind as the ones referred to as "vessels unto dishonour of wood and earth," then Paul is telling Timothy to purge himself from these believers (v. 21), so he can have the fuller ministry and life of power for God, thus illustrating SEPARATION from disorderly believers. Opinion is divided, however, on who the "great house" is.

   c. 2 Timothy 4:14-15. In the fourth chapter of 2 Timothy, Paul made his last message to his young friend. After mentioning his own departure from this life after a fruitful sojourn here, Paul names some of his friends who had been with him on different occasions. Demas had forsaken him, (2 Timothy 4:10), Crescens had left, and also Titus (4:10). Luke was with him; he asked for Mark to come with Timothy to Rome where Paul was a prisoner, and Tychicus went to Ephesus on Paul's command (2 Timothy 4:11-12).

In verses 14-15, Paul made mention of Alexander the coppersmith who did him much evil. Perhaps this is the same Alexander mentioned in 1 Timothy 1:20 along with Hymenaeus whom Paul delivered unto Satan; it may also be the one mentioned in Acts 19:33 in the riot at Ephesus. At any rate, since he is mentioned in the list of Paul's believing friends, it is possible that Alexander may have been a carnal, fleshly believer who caused Paul much grief.

If such is the case, Alexander pictures a disorderly believer from whom Paul wanted Timothy to be SEPARATE since he told him to beware of him (2 Timothy 4:15). Though the usual believer is not mentioned by Paul in such words and for such sins, yet many of Paul's fellow believers had to be rebuked on occasions by the apostle for disorderliness of the flesh and this man, Alexander, might have been one such believer who was walking after the flesh instead of after the spirit.

   d. Titus 3:8-11. The final passage of a doubtful sort concerning the SEPARATION from disorderly believers in the New Testament is found in Titus 3:8-11. Paul mentioned to Titus to maintain good works for profitable uses before the world (Titus 3:8). Then he mentioned that Titus was to avoid foolish questions and genealogies such as was the custom of some of the believers and even non-Christians of that day (Titus 3:9). These were unprofitable and vain (Titus 3:9b). Then Paul mentioned a man who is a heretic (Titus 3:10).

The question comes up as to whether this "heretic" mentioned in Titus 3:10 is a believer who is walking after the flesh, or a natural man who is living in the flesh. This word translated "heretic" merely meant one who had a particular opinion on matters or a member of a set of persons professing "particular principles or opinions." It may be translated as one who is a member of a "school, sect, party, or faction." This is quite different from the sense in which we use the word "heretic" today. Today we mean one who is usually a member of a non-Christian cult such as Christian Science or the like, where there is no gospel truth. Then, however, it is quite possible that this man may have been a believer who was merely taken up with idle speculation.

Further internal proof that this one may have been a believer is that Paul encouraged Titus to warn him twice, but after the first and second warning to REJECT him (Titus 3:10). This warning would be entirely apropos to a disorderly believer, though quite beyond the call of duty, it seems, if the person were just another unsaved religionist.

  2. New Testament SEPARATION Passages From Disorderly Believers That Are Clear. Regardless of the small doubt which may hang over the four above passages regarding the clear teaching of the New Testament regarding SEPARATION from disorderly believers, there are two passages which are without question in their teaching concerning this point.

  a. 1 Corinthians 5:1-13 Clearly Teaches SEPARATION From Disorderly Believers. In 1 Corinthians, Paul had to handle all sorts of carnality and sins in the Christian church.

  (1) The Sin Of Incest in 1 Corinthians 5. In chapter five of 1 Corinthians, Paul mentioned incestuous relations on the part of one of the Corinthian believers and his father's wife (1 Corinthians 5:1). This person is without doubt to be considered as a believer in the Lord Jesus Christ though walking after the flesh (cf. 1 Corinthians 5:1, 5, 11-12).

  (2) Paul Denounced The Corinthian Attitude Toward This Sin. Paul denounced the church at Corinth for being "puffed up" over this incident, rather than being mournful and repentant as they should have been. Paul wanted to deliver this one to Satan "for the destruction of the flesh" (1 Corinthians 5:5) that his spirit might be saved, so great was his sin in Paul's estimation. [G. Abbott-Smith, *A Manual Greek Lexicon of the New Testament*, p. 13].

  (3) The Difficulty of TOTAL Separation Or Contact With The World Of Sinners. Then Paul began to tell the Corinthians what to do about the one who had thus sinned against the Lord (1 Corinthians 5:7-13). He wanted them to purge out this leaven of sin so that the assembly at Corinth might remain a pure lump (1 Corinthians 5:7). Paul did not want the Corinthians to keep company with fornicators, but this did not mean worldly fornicators, or covetous, "or extortioners, or with idolaters; for then must ye needs go out of the world" (1 Corinthians 5:9-10). In the city of Corinth with such a wicked reputation for vice ant sins of all types, it would be impossible to SEPARATE themselves totally from all the fornicators of the world, for then they could hardly do any business in the stores and so forth.

(4) Paul Taught Clearly TOTAL SEPARATION From A disorderly Christian Fornicator or Similar Sinner. Paul's main criticism was that the believers should not have anything to do with the "fornicator" who is called a brother in Christ and who has not yet confessed his sin and been restored first to the Lord and then to the local church. This ban from fellowship also rests upon the disorderly believer who is covetous, an idolater, a railer, a drunkard, an extortioner and the like (I Corinthians 5:11). They are not even to eat with such believers until, it is supposed, they are repentant and restored to fellowship with the Lord. 2 Corinthians 2:6-11 mentioned that this fornicator among them was restored first to the Lord and then to the Corinthians and Paul. They are told to love him once again when this takes place, but not before (2 Corinthians 2:8). It is to "love" him in the fullest sense of full fellowship and restoration, that is, not in the sense of Christian "love" and care and concern.

b. 2 Thessalonians 3:6-15 Clearly Teaches SEPARATION From Disorderly Believers. The second clear passage regarding the SEPARATION of believers from other believers who walk disorderly is found in 2 Thessalonians 3:6-15.

(1) The General Problem Of Christian "disorderliness." In this section, Paul is discussing the general question of disorderliness in which the Thessalonian church had been engaged. Paul told them to WITHDRAW themselves from

every brother that walketh disorderly, and not after the tradition which he received of us (2 Thessalonians 3:6).

This was nothing short of a command.

(2) Paul's Example Of Orderliness. Paul then mentioned that he himself was not disorderly when among them (2 Thessalonians 3:7) but instead worked night and day so he would not have to live on the charity of any of the believers of Thessalonica (2 Thessalonians 3:8). This was all for the purpose of an example to these believers so that they too might work (2 Thessalonians 3:9) and if any did not wish to work he was not "to eat" (2 Thessalonians 3:10). Those who did not work were disorderly busybodies (2 Thessalonians 3:11).

(3) Paul Taught Clearly TOTAL SEPARATION From A Disorderly Christian In This Case. After mentioning the failures and disorderliness of some of the members of the Thessalonian church, Paul said if anyone did not obey Paul's orders just outlined, he should be noted [that is, named for all to see] and other orderly believers should SEPARATE themselves and have NO COMPANY with him that he might be ashamed (2

Thessalonians 3:14). Though SEPARATED from other believers, this. man should still be reckoned as a "brother" and should be gently admonished and warned so that he may in a later time be fully restored to the Lord and to the other believers of Thessalonica. This was to discourage and condemn the practice of laziness on the part of large numbers in the church who were becoming as leeches on the more industrious Christians.

CHAPTER VI
SUMMARY AND CONCLUSIONS

Before concluding such a study on Biblical teaching on SEPARATION, it will be in order to give a summary and some pertinent conclusions of each major section of the research.

I. SEPARATION REGARDING THINGS

A. SEPARATION Regarding Canaanite Ways And God's Ways.
    1. **Summary**. This section was divided into the reason for separation and the command for separation, in the area of SEPARATION from Canaanite ways. The section of SEPARATION unto God's ways was divided as to the reason for the separation and the command for the separation. One side was negative, and the other side positive.
    2. **Conclusions**. Israel was not to venture into agreements, deals, contracts, or associations of an unnecessary character with the Canaanite unbelievers nor were they to partake of their sinful ways. So the believer today, by application, is commanded by various portions of the New Testament in a direct way to remain SEPARATED **unto** God's will positively, while at the same time being in a position of SEPARATION **from**, negatively, the ways and compromising associations of the sinners that live all around him. This would prohibit contacts of a fellowship and associational nature from such apostate religious groups as the National Council of Churches, the world Council of Churches, the Consultation on Church Union, and the like. It would also prohibit contacts of a fellowship and associational nature, by extension, with such unbelieving persons as the Communists, other atheists, and similar unbelievers and false teachers.

B. SEPARATION Regarding Jewish Customs.
    1. **Summary**. SEPARATION regarding Jewish customs included five main topics: (1) SEPARATION regarding days, (2) SEPARATION regarding diet, (3) SEPARATION regarding property, (4) SEPARATION regarding disease and sanitation, and (5) SEPARATION regarding miscellaneous customs.
    2. **Conclusions**. Though these customs are for the most part directed specifically and primarily to the nation of Israel under her Old Testament economy, there are some principles that carry over to the age of grace as well. God has a priority on the believer's time, his diet, and his

property. Whatsoever things that are done in word or deed are supposedly to be done for the glory of the Lord Jesus Christ (Cf. 1 Corinthians 10:31), putting Him first and foremost in all activities of life. Just as God was interested that Israel be a SEPARATED people as to garments and dress, so He is interested in the believer's inner dress of a meek and quiet spirit as well (I Peter 3:4) as proper external garments and dress.

C. SEPARATION Regarding Money And Valuables.

1. Summary. The section regarding SEPARATION and money had three main divisions: (1) valuables refused, including the illustrations of Abram, Elisha and Peter; (2) valuables SEPARATED for special use, including money to build the tabernacle, firstfruits, tithes, and valuables presented to the Lord. (3) valuables, misused, including multiplication of gold and silver, multiplication of horses, and some other special cases of misuse.

2. Conclusions. The believer as he lives his life in the present evil world system occasionally has to learn how to say "no" to offers that look outwardly tempting, but that come from Satanic sources. He also has to learn to SEPARATE his time and money to be used as God sees fit, giving only to causes that are completely Biblical in principle and practice. The principal of putting God first in the life extends to the pocketbook as well as to other avenues of life, though the tithe is only a beginning to a godly program of giving under grace.

D. SEPARATION Regarding Places.

1. Summary. In the discussion of SEPARATION regarding places, there were three general fields of study taken up: (1) places to leave, including Ur, Sodom, and Egypt; (2) places to avoid, including Egypt, Mount Sinai, and the tabernacle; and (3) places to enter, including Canaan and Jerusalem.

2. Conclusions. Though most of the discussion of this section of the study was confined in illustration to the Old Testament, yet much of the truth in principal can be applied to the present day. There may be no places to "leave" in the same sense as Israel was to leave Egypt, for example, but there are certainly sinful and wicked places in the midst of this cursed world which are no places for the child of God to enter. Such places are to be avoided by all means. On the other hand, there are many positive places for the believer to go, including his church, Sunday school (especially separated, godly, Bible-centered churches and Sunday Schools which have no connection with the apostasy of our day), prayer meeting, the mission field or wherever else God leads a person in his witness for the Lord Jesus Christ, in accord with His Written Words. Too often the believer's life is ruined because he went into the wrong places and therefore mixed with the wrong people. It is a mistake to think the Christian can enter the strongholds of Satan and attempt to change

them for the better. God's way is for the believer to avoid such places, and to be SEPARATED from them.
  E. **SEPARATION Regarding Specific Sins.**
    1. **Summary.** In the discussion of SEPARATION regarding specific sins, four general points were discussed: (l) the call to separation from sin; (2) the sin of drink, including warnings about drink, bad examples about drink, and good examples about drink; (3) the sin of idolatry, including warnings about idolatry, and failures about idolatry; and (4) the sin of sensuality, including warnings about sensuality and failures about sensuality.
    2. **Conclusions.** The question of SEPARATION regarding specific sins is constant in its application. It is ageless in its scope, applying with equal vigor and force to Israel as to the church of the Lord Jesus Christ of this age and dispensation. The problem of sin comes from three main sources-- the world, the flesh, and the devil--but it is overcome by none other than the Holy Spirit of God Who indwells every born again believer in the Lord Jesus Christ. If the believer is walking in the Spirit, he will not be fulfilling the desires of the flesh with all its sins (Galatians 5:16), but will seek to be SEPARATE from these sins.

II. SEPARATION REGARDING MARRIAGE

  A. **The Dispensational Aspects Of Marriage.**
    1. **Summary.** In the discussion of the dispensational aspects of marriage, three general points were brought out: (l) the dispensations defined, including innocence, conscience, human government, promise, law, grace, and kingdom; (2) the dispensations involved, including innocence, conscience, promise, law, and grace; and (3) the applicability of marriage teaching, including the facts that marriage occurred in every dispensation, marriage is like ethics, and marriage principles are constant.
    2. **Conclusions.** As has been pointed out by one of the divisions on the study of marriage, marriage is like ethics, that is, its principles are constant for every age and situation--in principle, if not in actual details. More Christian homes are ruined and wrecked because of miscalculations in the realm of marriage than for perhaps any other reasons. These problems are just as much a part of the present dispensation as they were of any past age.
  B. **Examples of SEPARATED Marriage.**
    1. **Summary.** The discussion of examples of SEPARATED marriages was divided into two sections: (1) the lessons from Eden, including the purpose of a wife, the nature of a wife, and the number of wives; and (2) examples of SEPARATED marriages, including the Old Testament examples of Moses' parents and Elimelech and Naomi, and the New Testament examples

of Zacharias and Elizabeth, Joseph and Mary, and Aquila and Priscilla.

2. Conclusions. Even today, God wants the believers to be diligent in their observance of SEPARATION in the marriage bond, even as were the above-named examples from the sacred Words of God. The marriage of Christians with other Christians is to be the practice of the present day believers in order to preserve the purity and integrity of the home so that God can bless the family wholeheartedly as the two parents bring up their children in the nurture and admonition of the Lord, walking in God's will.

C. Marriages With Heathen.

1. Summary. The division of marriages with heathen are divided into three main sections: (1) teaching against marriages with heathen, including; (a) the patriarchal teaching of Abram and Isaac, (b) the pre-exilic teaching of Moses, Joshua, and Samson's parents, and © the post-exilic teaching of Ezra and Nehemiah; (2) reasons against marriages with the heathen, including (a) reasons that concern God such as so they would not transgress, so their hearts would not turn away, and so they would not commit idolatry, and (b) reasons that concern man such as so the Lord would drive out the Canaanites, so the heathen would not be as snares, and Israel would be blessed in the land, and so their children would speak purely; and (3) instances of marriages with heathen, in the times of the patriarchs, in the time of the wanderings, in the time of the Judges, in the time of the kings, and in the time of the post-exile.

2. Conclusions. The fact of the Israelite marriages with so very many heathen nations serves as a warning to the believer of today as he attempts to choose his mate in these sinful days. There is just as much teaching pertaining to the sinfulness of marrying an unsaved person today, as in the case of Israel. With Israel, however, there were very clear teachings, I feel, of not only spiritual purity, but racial purity and also language purity as reasons against such inter-marriage with heathen, strange races, and people.

The problem that faces the present-day believer is not the teachings on this subject, but the practice of these teachings in the daily life. Marriage with the unsaved will just as much be a snare to the child of God today as in the former ages. The language of such a mixed marriage will no doubt not long remain pure either. Not so much from the standpoint of actual dialect, as from the standpoint of vulgarity, cursing, swearing, and even blasphemy that may come from the mouth of the unsaved member of such a mis-matched home. After the birth of children into this family, these words of vileness and sin go into the ears, not only of the saved mate, but also the very souls and hearts of the little ones whom God has given the couple to raise for him.

Rather than basing love and marriage upon mere shallow and superficial grounds among believers, there should, on the contrary, be a serious attempt to find the will of the Lord in the matter--certainly it could never be taken as the will of God to marry some unconverted, lost, Hell-bound sinner, no matter how seemly they appear to be. Marriage must be SEPARATED from the lost and unto the Lord's will and ways in His Words.

    D. New Testament Teaching On SEPARATED Marriage.

        1. Summary. New Testament teaching on SEPARATED marriage was divided into three parts: (1) apparent exceptions to SEPARATED marriage, including 1 Corinthians 7, and 1 Peter 3; (2) Scriptures implying SEPARATED marriage, including 1 Timothy 3:11, 1 Peter 3:7, and 2 Corinthians 6:14-18; and (3) Scriptures demanding SEPARATED marriage, including Ephesians 5:22-33 and Revelation 19:7-9.

        2. Conclusions. It Is not left up to the individual believer to decide whether or not God's principles pertaining to SEPARATED marriages pertain in the present time as well as in Israel's age. These facts are revealed within the pages of the New Testament Scriptures both by the apparent exceptional; the implications of several Scriptures, and the clear teachings of other verses. Far from contradicting the norm for SEPARATED marriage; 1 Corinthians 7 and 1 Peter 3 really agree in their insistence that the believer is to marry only other believers in this age. These two passages had reference to cases when one of the two believers had been saved after the marriage. The picture of the Lord Jesus Christ and the church which is His body, is the height of Scripture illustration of SEPARATED marriage. He has chosen for Himself a holy and elect bride who one day is to be without spot or wrinkle or any such thing--the believer living in the earth below is to do the same thing as he chooses the one who is to dwell with him until death parts them both. All of this argues for a SEPARATED marriage of believers with believers.

III. SEPARATION REGARDING UNBELIEVERS

    A. Israel's SEPARATION Regarding The Canaanites.

        1. Summary. In the discussion of Israel's SEPARATION regarding the Canaanites, three things were brought out: (l) teaching regarding the Canaanites, including the fact that the Canaanites were to be removed, and Israel's instructions; (2) Obedience to the teaching both in Moses' time and Joshua's time; and (3) disobedience to the teaching regarding their removal, covenants, fellowship, marriage, and idolatry.

        2. Conclusions. Unbelievers are to have no intimate hold on the believer of today, any more than they were to attract the Israelites who were intimately associated with the wicked Canaanites of old. There should be a distinctive SEPARATION in this regard from the unbelievers of today. Not that it is possible to remove the unbelievers from contact with believers (as was possible in the land of Canaan), but avoidance of alliances and leagues with the unsaved around the believer is a necessary step, if he is to please God. This step should first be preceded, however, by the step of entire SEPARATION unto God.

There should be a forsaking of any alliance with the National Council of Churches, the World Council of Churches, the Consultation on Church Union, and other such ungodly and apostate-controlled, satanic religious groups. It is also sinful, wicked, and a violation of the Holy Words of God for a minister or a layman to remain identified in any of the apostate-controlled churches such as are in these groups mentioned above. Men like evangelist Billy Graham are committing grievous sin against the God of Heaven by their unscriptural and unholy alliances with apostates, modernists, and high-priests of Hell in various ways. Many of the NEO-EVANGELICALS are following Graham's false, ungodly, wicked, heathen ways of compromise with the Words of God, and are going to suffer the penalty of God's wrath upon their disobedience, even as disobedient Israel suffered it when He could bear it no longer. Men such as those in the leadership of the NATIONAL ASSOCIATION OF EVANGELICALS who are also linked with such apostate groups as the Presbyterian Church in the U.S. which permits apostates to be within this denomination, and in the other apostate-controlled groups like the United Presbyterian Church in the U.S.A., are also sinning. All individuals and laymen alike who remain in unholy and unscriptural alliances with the United Methodist Church, the Protestant Episcopal church, and the other NCC/WCC and/or COCU churches are willfully violating the clear teaching of the Bible and will be judged by the Lord one way or another.

  B. **Examples of SEPARATION Regarding Unbelievers.**

    1. **Summary.** Failure in SEPARATION regarding unbelievers made mention of four major time periods: (1) failure in the time of the patriarchs, including Abram, Lot, Esau, Dinah, Joseph's brethren, Judah, and Jacob; (2) Failure in the time of Moses and the Judges, including Moses, Israel, Samson, and Elimelech and Naomi; (3) Failure in the time of the kings, including Saul, David, Solomon, Abijam, Asa, Ahab, Jehoshaphat, Ahaziah, Amaziah, Uzziah, Ahaz, Hezekiah, and Josiah; (4) Failure in the time of the post-exile, including Ezra's people, Nehemiah's people, and Esther.

    2. **Conclusions.** The Canaanites were not the only unbelievers that the children of Israel were to be SEPARATED from. All the unsaved with whom they came in contact were equally taboo from Israel's inner circle of friends, though God's people transgressed this part of His plan with considerable frequency. Leagues were made between Israel and ungodly kings, bargains were sealed with Judah and some of the most pagan nations of the ancient world--in short, mixtures of all sorts and varieties were the rule in the pages of God's Words with but few exceptions.

In the present time, the distinctions of SEPARATION from unbelievers still holds, though from the way Evangelist Billy Graham is carrying on, you wouldn't know it. All too often the tendency is to join the ranks of worldly groups for one reason or another, thus binding the individual to a common goal with these infidels. Billy Graham in making such unholy, ungodly, sinful, and wicked alliances of various kinds, including the Buddhism of Mr. Ky, the Judaism of the architects of his Herod's temple, the NCCism and apostasy of those with whom he shares his "MARCHES" platforms, his fraternization with Roman Catholicism in common causes again in the picket-march-rally syndrome which seems more and more to be his as he searches for new ways of getting money.

This union, however, is not to be blessed of God, though sometimes He blesses in spite of it. The links with modernism that have been made by so many professed believers are amazing as to frequency today. There seems to be little care whether or not the church members with which one is associated are saved or lost, on their way to Heaven or Hell. These things are important to God.

Though it is very difficult to draw lines and boundaries on the question of fellowship with unbelievers, the general principles are crystal-clear as outlined by the failures on the part of Biblical characters to stay out of unholy alliances with the heathen. Duty and love to God and God's people supersedes all alliances with the wicked of this earth--even the religiously wicked.

C. **Success In SEPARATION Regarding Unbelievers.**

1. **Summary.** Success in SEPARATION regarding unbelievers included the following divisions of study (1) success in the time of the patriarchs, including Enoch, Noah, Abram, Jacob, and Joseph; (2) success in the time of the kings, including Asa, Jehoshaphat, Elijah, John, Jehoida, and Hezekiah; (3) success in the time of the exile, including Daniel, Shadrach, Meshach, and Abednego, and Jeremiah, and (4) success in the time of the post-exile, including Ezra, Nehemiah, and Mordecai.

2. **Conclusions.** Though the majority of the Bible characters mentioned in the Scriptures had varying degrees of unholy alliance with apostate unbelievers, there were a few that SEPARATED themselves wholly unto the Lord and from these wicked men and women around them as required by God's Words. They were able to live above the tide, daring to be different in the midst of a world that cried out for conformity. So the believer today is called upon to be different, in the good sense. He is to fellowship with believers and his God, going to the unsaved only for essential things of life and in order to win them to the Lord Jesus Christ before it is too late.

D. New Testament SEPARATION Regarding Unbelievers.
1. Summary. Four divisions of New Testament SEPARATION regarding unbelievers were made: (1) SEPARATION in the New and Old Testaments compared, regarding the people concerned, the place, and God's purpose; (2) SEPARATION in the time of the Lord Jesus Christ, including the Lord Jesus Christ Himself, the twelve apostles, Peter, and the teaching in the Upper Room; (3) SEPARATION in the book of Acts, including both Paul and Peter, and (4) SEPARATION in the Epistles and Revelation, including Paul's letters, the general epistles, and Revelation.

2. Conclusions. SEPARATION from unbelievers is amply illustrated for the believer in the pages of the New Testament so that there is little room for speculating with regard to it. The Lord Jesus Christ affords a good example of His dealings with the unsaved in that He was always trying to meet their need spiritually and for Him, even physically because of His miraculous power and the need to show "signs" that men might believe (John 20:29-31), yet He remained absolutely "SEPARATE from sinners" (Hebrews 7:26) in the sense of partaking of their ways and sins. This pattern is urged upon the believers also, that they might be as their Lord was in all things, trying to win them one by one without conformity to the world (Cf. Romans 12:1-2).

IV. SEPARATION REGARDING DISORDERLY BELIEVERS

A. Definition of Terms.
1. Summary. In the section on definition of terms, such words as "believers," "disorderly," "orderly," and "SEPARATION" were taken up.

2. Conclusions. Though the Words "believers" usually has reference to a present-day believer of this age, it has been thought proper to think of God's Old Testament saints that were under the covenant promises as "believers" too. Though they were not believers in the Lord Jesus Christ as we are today, they nevertheless had faith in the One who was to come and their salvation ultimately rested on the Lamb of God's finished work of the cross. Some of these Old Testament believers were disorderly (in violation of God's clearly revealed will) and also were orderly, just as some today are disorderly and some orderly. It is my sincere conviction that those believers who are disobedient to God and His Words in refusing to SEPARATE from unbelievers according to the clear commands to do such in His Words (Cf. 2 Corinthians 6 14--7:1; Ephesians 5:11, etc.) are, by definition DISORDERLY BELIEVERS and other believers should SEPARATE from them in matters of church fellowship and alliances until they become OBEDIENT and ORDERLY believers and obey God's Words in these matters.

B. **SEPARATION Regarding Orderly Believers.**
1. **Summary.** SEPARATION regarding orderly believers was divided into four parts: (1) Bezaleel; (2) the Nazarites, including rules for Nazarites, Samson the Nazarite, and failures of Nazarites; (3) the Levites, including (a) the regular Levites as to their SEPARATION, their general duties, and their special duties, and (b) the priests, as to their priestly family of Aaron, and the high priest; and (4) the prophets, including their purpose, their reception, and their failures.
2. **Conclusions.** In the general subject of SEPARATION regarding believers, there are some occasions in the Old Testament as well as in the New, for God to pick out special believers that He wishes to use in a special way. The builder of the tabernacle, Bezaleel, was that way; so were the Nazarites, the Levites, and the prophets. In the present time too, God is calling out from the general group of believer-priests those who have the special gifts of God of teaching, pastoring, evangelism and the like, and putting them into a special place of usefulness for Himself. It behooves every such man, called for God's purpose, to exercise this gift to the greatest capacity.

C. **Old Testament SEPARATION Regarding Disorderly Believers.**
1, **Summary**. Old Testament SEPARATION regarding disorderly believers was divided into two parts: (1) SEPARATION by leaving, including (a) the disorderly leaving the orderly as in the case of Cain, Lot, Hagar, lepers, manslayers, and unclean persons, and (b) the orderly leaving the disorderly, as in the case of Abram, Jacob, Joseph, Levites, Moses and Aaron, Moses and the Judges of Israel, David, and Israel; and (2) SEPARATION by death, including references to a believer's being "cut off," and also to his being "put to death" in plain language.
2. **Conclusions.** The Old Testament had its illustrations of the believers who were orderly belay SEPARATED from the disorderly believers. The chief of these types of SEPARATION was by death for various sins that were worthy thereof. No less than 15 sins were punishable by that person's being "cut off" from his people, and as many as 20 sins were punished by death. God does not fool with believers who toy with sin. They must be SEPARATED from the rest of the believers either by leaving or, in the Old Testament at least, by death itself.

D. **New Testament SEPARATION Regarding Disorderly Believers.**
1. **Summary.** The division on New Testament SEPARATION regarding disorderly believers took up two things: (1) a definition of terms, including "believers," "orderly." "disorderly," and "separation," and (2) passages on SEPARATION from disorderly believers, including disputed passages and clear passages.

2. Conclusions. Even in the New Testament there is laid down the principle of SEPARATION from disorderly believers. When believers sin, they must make it right with God by instant confession of all known sin (1 John 1:9). If this is not done, that believer is out of fellowship with God. In certain types of disorderly conduct, the disorderly ones are to be banned from fellowship from the assembly until such a time as they make confession of that sin to God and are restored both to the Lord and to man. If more of the churches today would practice the principle laid down in God's Words of SEPARATION from certain classes of disorderly believers, there would be less carnality among believers, there would be less chance of modernism creeping into churches, and most important of all, there would be far less talk on the part of the unsaved about hypocrites in the churches. Members who lived in open and reproachful sin would no longer be members of the churches if Pauline methods of operation were followed minutely (cf. 1 Corinthians 5:1-13).

As was said before in the Conclusions of a previous section, one of the clearest and most serious sins of today's DISORDERLY believers, is the sin of disobedience to God and His Words when it comes to SEPARATION from ungodly, lost, unsaved, modernists and apostates. Such a believer who stays within the apostasy of the NCC, the WCC, the COCU, or other similar groups and the denominations that are within this network of groups, is certainly, by application, a DISORDERLY BELIEVER. The commands of God for such sinful and DISORDERLY people come into effect, and we, if we are to be obedient to God, are to shun such DISORDERLY believers; we are to have no fellowship with them in religious matters; and we are to expose them and mark them and note them as a warning to others. When they repent, and realize that they have been sinning in the matter of fellowship with unbelievers (2 Corinthians 6:14--7:1), the orderly believers who are obedient in these matters, are to receive them back into fellowship once again, and to warmly receive them as "orderly" once again. By these definitions, Christians who are orderly today, have an obligation to SEPARATE from disorderly believers today until they repent and change their disobedient ways.

Having cited some 1,896 VERSES from the Bible, God's Holy Words, in this "BIBLICAL TEACHING ON SEPARATION," I can say with all the conviction which comes from absolute faith in God's plenarily, verbally, inspired and hence infallible and inerrant Words that GOD IS A SEPARATIST! If God is a SEPARATIST, why aren't you???!!!

INDEX OF WORDS AND PHRASES

1 Chronicles 11-13, 17, 49, 52, 65, 66
1 Corinthians 14, 23, 24, 38-40, 60, 80-82, 86, 89, 94
1 John 61, 78, 94
1 Kings 10, 14, 18, 20-22, 32, 36, 37, 46, 49-51, 55, 67, 68, 72, 78
1 Peter 39, 40, 89
1 Samuel 14, 22, 24, 49, 72
1 Timothy 40, 79, 80, 89
1,896 Bible verses .... 1, i, 6
1954 .... ii, 3
1971 .... ii, 3, 50
1997 .... ii, 3, 51
2 Chronicles 10, 11, 17, 20, 23, 24, 37, 46, 50-52, 55, 56, 65-67, 78
2 Corinthians 40, 42, 58, 60, 82, 89, 92, 94
2 John 61
2 Kings 10-12, 16, 18, 23, 24, 36, 37, 46, 52, 56, 67, 68
2 Samuel 11, 12, 24, 49, 78
2 Timothy 80
A.C.C.C 5
Acts 11, 16, 24, 26, 30, 48, 60, 80, 85, 87, 89, 92
American Council of Christian Churches 4, 5
Amos 65
animals 7, 13-15, 28, 54
believers 3, 7-10, 16, 19, 26, 29, 32, 39-61, 63-65, 67, 69-72, 74, 75, 78-83, 85, 88-94
Bible Induction Work Sheet 6
Bible our only authority 4
Biblical separation 3, 8, 13, 69
blood 3, 14, 20, 58, 66, 73
Canaanite ways 7, 9, 10, 85
Canaanites 7, 9-11, 30-32, 35, 37, 43-46, 88-90
Colossians 24
compromise 50, 51, 69, 70, 90
Consultation on Church Union 6, 85, 90
Daniel 14, 23, 56, 57, 68, 91

days 8, 12, 13, 22, 29, 35, 52, 65, 67, 70, 74, 85, 88
disorderly 7, 8, 63, 64, 67-83, 92-94
dispensation 7, 25-27, 41, 59, 72, 87
dispensational aspects of marriage 7, 25, 87
dispensations 25-27, 87
Dr. John R. Rice 8, 63, 69
Dr. Lewis Sperry Chafer 6
Egypt 9, 10, 19, 22, 29, 33, 34, 45, 46, 48-50, 52, 57, 58, 65,
66, 70-72, 86
Ephesians 9, 10, 24, 27, 40-42, 60, 89, 92
Esther 38, 53, 58, 90
Exodus 13, 17, 19, 20, 22, 24-26, 29, 30, 32, 34, 43, 44, 48,
64, 66, 71-73, 75, 77
Ezekiel 11, 16, 17, 21, 23, 24, 52, 68, 69
Ezra 11, 31-33, 37, 38, 53, 57, 67, 68, 88, 90, 91
failures of some prophets 68, 69
G. Aiken Taylor 6
Genesis 16, 18, 19, 22-26, 28, 30, 33, 34, 43, 46-48, 54, 55,
70-72
gold 17, 18, 50, 52, 77, 80, 86
Haggai 67
Hebrews 24, 59, 92
horses 17, 19, 23, 50, 51, 86
Hosea 24, 68
Isaiah 19, 21, 24, 50, 52, 56, 68, 69
James 24, 61, 79
Jeremiah 11, 22-24, 57, 67-69, 91
Jewish customs 9, 13, 85
Job 66, 68
John 8, 16, 24, 29, 41, 59-61, 63, 69, 76, 78, 91, 92, 94
Joshua 11, 12, 14, 15, 17, 20, 22, 24, 31, 32, 35, 43-46, 77, 88,
89
Jude 24
Judges 21, 22, 24, 27, 29, 31, 32, 35, 36, 46, 48, 65, 72, 77,
88, 90, 93
Lamentations 24, 65, 68, 69
Leviticus 10-15, 20-24, 26, 34, 44, 66, 70, 73-76
Luke 24, 26, 29, 59, 80
Malachi 17, 67
Mark 25, 29, 49, 59, 80, 94
marriages with the heathen 25, 30, 31, 33-38, 88

Matthew 24, 58, 59
Micah 68, 69
money 7, 9, 16-18, 54, 68, 86, 91
money and valuables 9, 16, 18, 86
N.A.E. 4-6, 70
N.C.C. 5, 6
N.C.C. apostasy 6
National Association of Evangelicals 4, 5, 70, 90
negative separation 4, 12
Nehemiah 11, 31, 33, 36, 38, 53, 57, 68, 88, 91
neo-evangelicals 10, 90
New Testament separation regarding disorderly believers 8, 63, 93
New Testament separation regarding unbelievers 7, 43, 92
Numbers 15, 17, 21, 22, 24, 29, 34, 43, 44, 48, 64-66, 70-76, 83
Old Testament separation regarding disorderly believers 8, 63, 69, 72, 93
Philippians 3, 42, 61
positive separation 4, 12
Presbyterian Church in the U.S. 6, 90
prophets 21, 26, 52, 55, 64, 67-69, 76, 93
Proverbs 24
Psalms 11, 23
Revelation 22-24, 26, 31, 41, 60, 61, 89, 92
Rice 8, 63, 69
Romans 14, 23, 24, 60, 92
Ruth 29, 36, 49
separated marriage 7, 25, 27, 29, 30, 33, 34, 38-42, 87, 89
separated marriages 7, 25, 27, 29, 31, 87, 89
separation from 4, 5, 9, 10, 14-16, 19-23, 44-61, 63, 64, 71, 78-83, 85, 87, 91-94
separation in marriage 26, 27
separation regarding disorderly believers 7, 8, 63, 69, 72, 78, 93
separation regarding marriage 7, 25-27, 43, 46, 53
separation regarding orderly believers 8, 63, 64, 93
separation regarding things................................. 7, 9, 25
separation regarding unbelievers 7, 43, 55, 90-92
separation unto 4, 11, 12, 48, 54, 65, 85, 90
silver 17, 18, 47, 50-52, 77, 80, 86

specific sins 7, 9, 20, 21, 87
success in separation regarding unbelievers 7, 43, 91
summary and conclusions 8, 85
Sword of the Lord 8, 63, 69
Systematic Theology 6
TABLE OF CONTENTS iii
The Biblical Teaching on Separation 3
Titus 80, 81
valuables 9, 16-18, 86
World Council of Churches 4, 6, 85, 90
Zechariah 21, 52, 67, 68

About the Author

The author of this book, Dr. D. A. Waite, received a B.A. (Bachelor of Arts) in classical Greek and Latin from the University of Michigan in 1948, a Th.M. (Master of Theology), with high honors, in New Testament Greek Literature and Exegesis from Dallas Theological Seminary in 1952, an M.A. (Master of Arts) in Speech from Southern Methodist University in 1953, a Th.D. (Doctor of Theology), with honors, in Bible Exposition from Dallas Theological Seminary in 1955, and a Ph.D. in Speech from Purdue University in 1961. He holds both New Jersey and Pennsylvania teacher certificates in Greek and Language Arts.

He has been a teacher in the areas of Greek, Hebrew, Bible, Speech, and English for over thirty-five years in ten schools, including one junior high, one senior high, four Bible institutes, two colleges, two universities, and one seminary. He served his country as a Navy Chaplain for five years on active duty; pastored three churches; was Chairman and Director of the Radio and Audio-Film Commission of the American Council of Christian Churches; since 1969, has been Founder, President, and Director of THE BIBLE FOR TODAY; since 1978, has been President of the DEAN BURGON SOCIETY; has produced over 800 other studies, books, audio cassettes, CD's, VCR's, or DVD's on various topics; and is heard on a thirty-minute weekly program, IN DEFENSE OF TRADITIONAL BIBLE TEXTS, on radio, and streaming on the Internet at BibleForToday.org, 24/7/365.

Dr. and Mrs. Waite have been married since 1948; they have four sons, one daughter, and, at present, eight grand-children, and eleven great-grandchildren. Since October 4, 1998, he has been the Pastor of the Bible For Today Baptist Church in Collingswood, New Jersey.

Order Blank (p. 1)

Name:_____

Address:_____

City & State:_____Zip:_____

Credit Card #:_____Expires:_____

Latest Books

[ ] Send *Biblical Separation* By Dr. D. A. Waite (130 pp. perfect Bound ($15.00 + $7.00 S&H)
[ ] Send *The Sixth 200 Questions Answered* By Dr. D. A. Waite (188 pp. perfect bound $15.00 + $7.00 S&H)
[ ] Send The Fifth 200 Questions Answered By Dr. D. A. Waite (150 pp. perfect bound $15.00 + $7.00 S&H)
[ ] Send *The Fourth 200 Questions Answered* By Dr. D. A. Waite (168 pp. perfect bound $15.00 + $7.00 S&H)
[ ] Send *The Third 200 Questions Answered* By Dr. D. A. Waite (180 pp. perfect bound $15.00 + $7.00 S&H)
[ ] Send *The Second 200 Questions Answered* By Dr. D. A. Waite (178 pp. perfect bound $15.00 + $7.00 S&H)
[ ] Send *The First 200 Questions Answered By Dr. D. A. Waite* (184 pp. perfect bound $12.00 + $7.00 S&H)
[ ] Send *A Critical Answer to James Price's King James Only-ism* By Pastor D. A. Waite, 184pp, perfect bound ($11+$7 S&H)
[ ] Send *The KJB's Superior Hebrew & Greek Words* by Pastor D. A. Waite, 104 pp., perfect bound ($10+$7 S&H)
[ ] Send *Soulwinning's Versions-Perversions* by Pastor D. A. Waite, booklet, 28 pp. ($6+$5 S&H) fully indexed
[ ] Send *2 Timothy--Preaching Verse by Verse*, by Pastor D. A. Waite, 250 pages, perfect bound ($11+$7 S&H) fully indexed.
[ ] Send *A Critical Answer to God's Word Preserved* by Pastor D. A. Waite, 192 pp. perfect bound ($11.00+$7.00 S&H)
[ ] Send *Daily Bible Blessings* By Yvonne Waite ($20.00+$8 S&H)
[ ] Send *Revelation–Preaching Verse By Verse* By Dr. D. A. Waite ($50+$10 S&H--1030 pages.

Send or Call Orders to:
THE BIBLE FOR TODAY
900 Park Ave., Collingswood, NJ 08108
Phone: 856-854-4452; FAX:--2464; Orders: 1-800 JOHN 10:9

Order Blank (p. 2)

Name:_____

Address:_____

City & State:_____Zip:_____

Credit Card #:_____Expires:_____

[ ] Send *The Occult Connections of Gail Riplinger* by Dr. Phil Stringer ($12.00 + $7.00 S&H).

[ ] Send *A WARNING!! On Gail Riplinger's KJB & Multiple Inspiration HERESY*, 133 pp. by Pastor DAW ($12+$7S&H)

[ ] Send *Who Is Gail Riplinger?* 146 pp. by Aleithia O'Brien ($12.00 + $7.00)

[ ] *The Messianic Claims Of Gail A. Riplinger*, By Dr. Phil Stringer, 108 pp., perfect bound ($12.00 + $7.00 S&H)

[ ] Send Husband-Loving Lessons, by Yvonne S. Waite; $25 + $7.00 S&H A very valuable marriage manual

[ ] Send *8,000 Differences Between Textus Receptus & Critical Text* by Dr.J.A. Moorman, 544 pp., hd.back ($20+$7 S&H)

[ ] *Early Manuscripts, Church Fathers, & the Authorized Version* by Dr. Jack Moorman, $20+$7 S&H. Hardback

[ ] Send *The LIE That Changed the Modern World* by Dr. H. D. Williams ($16+$7 S&H) Hardback book

[ ] Send *With Tears in My Heart* by Gertrude G. Sanborn. Hardback 414 pp. ($25+$7 S&H) 400 Christian Poems

Preaching Verse by Verse Books

[ ] Send *2 Timothy--Preaching Verse by Verse*, by Pastor D. A. Waite, 250 pages, hardback ($11+$7 S&H) fully indexed.

[ ] Send *1 Timothy--Preaching Verse by Verse*, by Pastor D. A.Waite, 288 pages, hardback ($14+$7 S&H) fully indexed.

More Preaching Verse by Verse Books

[ ] Send *Romans--Preaching Verse by Verse* by Pastor D. A. Waite 736 pp. Hardback ($25+$7 S&H) fully indexed

Send or Call Orders to:
THE BIBLE FOR TODAY
900 Park Ave., Collingswood, NJ 08108
Phone: 856-854-4452; FAX:--2464; Orders: 1-800 JOHN 10:9
E-Mail Orders: BFT@BibleForToday.org; Credit Cards OK

BIBLICAL SEPARATION By Pastor D. A. Waite, Th.D., Ph.D. 101

Order Blank (p. 3)

Name:_____

Address:_____

City & State:_____Zip:_____

Credit Card #:_____Expires:_____
[ ] Send *Colossians & Philemon--Preaching Verse by Verse* by Pastor D. A. Waite ($12+$7 S&H) hardback, 240 pages
[ ] Send *First Peter--Preaching Verse By Verse* by Pastor D. A. Waite ($10+$7 S&H) hardback, 176 pages
[ ] Send *Philippians--Preaching Verse by Verse* by Pastor D. A. Waite ($10+$7 S&H) hardback, 176 pages
[ ] Send *Ephesians--Preaching Verse by Verse* by Pastor D. A. Waite ($12+$7 S&H) hardback, 224 pages
[ ] Send *Galatians--Preaching Verse By Verse* by Pastor D. A. Waite ($13+$7 S&H) hardback, 216 pages

Books on Bible Texts & Translations
[ ] Send *Defending the King James Bible* by DAW ($12+$7 S&H) A hardback book, indexed with study questions
[ ] Send *BJU's Errors on Bible Preservation* by Dr. D. A. Waite, 110 pages, paperback ($8+$7 S&H) fully indexed
[ ] Send *Fundamentalist Deception on Bible Preservation* by Dr.Waite, ($8+$4 S&H), paperback, fully indexed
[ ] Send *Fundamentalist MIS-INFORMATION on Bible Versions* by Dr. Waite ($7+$5 S&H) perfect bound, 136 pages
[ ] Send *Fundamentalist Distortions on Bible Versions* by Dr.Waite ($7+$4 S&H) A perfect bound book, 80 pages
[ ] Send *Fuzzy Facts From Fundamentalists* by Dr. D. A. Waite ($8.00 + $7.00 S&H)

More Books on Bible Texts & Translations
[ ] Send *Foes of the King James Bible Refuted* by DAW ($9 +$7 S&H) A perfect bound book, 164 pages in length
[ ] Send *Central Seminary Refuted on Bible Versions* by Dr. Waite ($10+$7 S&H) A perfect bound book, 184 pages

Send or Call Orders to:
THE BIBLE FOR TODAY
900 Park Ave., Collingswood, NJ 08108
Phone: 856-854-4452; FAX:--2464; Orders: 1-800 JOHN 10:9
E-Mail Orders: BFT@BibleForToday.org; Credit Cards OK

Order Blank (p. 4)

Name:_____

Address:_____
)
City & State:_____Zip:_____

Credit Card #:_____Expires:_____

[ ] Send *The Case for the King James Bible* by DAW ($8 +$5 S&H) A perfect bound book, 112 pages in length
[ ] Send *Theological Heresies of Westcott and Hort* by Dr. D. A. Waite, ($8+$5 S&H) A printed booklet
[ ] Send *Westcott's Denial of Resurrection*, Dr. Waite ($8+$5)
[ ] Send *Four Reasons for Defending KJB* by DAW ($4+$3)

More Books on Texts & Translations

[ ] Send *Holes in the Holman Christian Standard Bible* by Dr. Waite ($6+$4 S&H) A printed booklet, 40 pages
[ ] Send *Contemporary Eng. Version Exposed*, DAW ($6+$4)
[ ] Send *NIV Inclusive Language Exposed* by DAW ($7+$5)
[ ] Send *24 Hours of KJB Seminar* (4 DVD's) by DAW ($50.00) + $10.00 S&H

Books By Dr. Jack Moorman

[ ] Send Manuscript Digest of the N.T. (721 pp.) By Dr. Jack Moorman, copy-machine bound ($50+$10.00 S&H)
[ ] *Early Manuscripts, Church Fathers, & the Authorized Version* by Dr. Jack Moorman, $20+$7 S&H. Hardback
[ ] Send *Forever Settled--Bible Documents & History Survey* by Dr. Jack Moorman, $20+$7 S&H. Hardback book
[ ] Send *When the KJB Departs from the So-Called "Majority Text"* By Dr. Jack Moorman ($17.00 + $7.00 S&H)

More Books By Dr. Jack Moorman

[ ] Send *Missing in Modern Bibles--Nestle/Aland/NIV Errors* by Dr. Jack Moorman, $8+$7 S&H
[ ] Send *The Doctrinal Heart of the Bible--Removed from Modern Versions* by Dr. Jack Moorman, VCR, $15 +$7 S&H

Send or Call Orders to:
THE BIBLE FOR TODAY
900 Park Ave., Collingswood, NJ 08108
Phone: 856-854-4452; FAX:--2464; Orders: 1-800 JOHN 10:9
E-Mail Orders: BFT@BibleForToday.org; Credit Cards OK

BIBLICAL SEPARATION By Pastor D. A. Waite, Th.D., Ph.D. **103**

Order Blank (p. 5)

Name:_____

Address:_____

City & State:_____Zip:_____

Credit Card #:_____Expires:_____
[ ] Send *Modern Bibles--The Dark Secret* by Dr. Jack Moorman, $5+$4 S&H
[ ] Send *Samuel P. Tregelles--The Man Who Made the Critical Text Acceptable to Bible Believers* by Dr. Moorman ($5+$3)
[ ] Send *8,000 Differences Between TR & CT* by Dr. Jack Moorman [$20 + $7.00 S&H] a hardback book

Books By or About Dean Burgon
[ ] Send *The Revision Revised* by Dean Burgon ($25 + $7 S&H) A hardback book, 640 pages in length
[ ] Send *356 Doctrinal Errors in the NIV & Other Modern Versions*, 100-large-pages, $10.00+$7 S&H
[ ] Send *The Last 12 verses of Mark* by Dean Burgon ($15+$7 S&H) A hardback book 400 pages
[ ] Send *The Traditional Text* hardback by Burgon ($15+$5 S&H) A hardback book, 384 pages in length
[ ] Send *Causes of Corruption* by Burgon ($16+$5 S&H) A hardback book, 360 pages in length

More Books By or About Dean Burgon
[ ] Send *Inspiration and Interpretation*, Dean Burgon ($25+$7 S&H) A hardback book, 610 pages in length
[ ] Send *Burgon's Warnings on Revision* by DAW ($7+$5 S&H) A perfect bound book, 120 pages in length
[ ] Send *Westcott & Hort's Greek Text & Theory Refuted by Burgon's Revision Revised--Summarized* by Dr. D. A. Waite ($7.00+$5 S&H), 120 pages, perfect bound
[ ] Send *Dean Burgon's Confidence in KJB* by DAW ($5+$4)
[ ] Send *Vindicating Mark 16:9-20* by Dr. Waite ($5+$4S&H)

Send or Call Orders to:
THE BIBLE FOR TODAY
900 Park Ave., Collingswood, NJ 08108
Phone: 856-854-4452; FAX:--2464; Orders: 1-800 JOHN 10:9
E-Mail Orders: BFT@BibleForToday.org; Credit Cards OK

Order Blank (p. 6)

Name:_____

Address:_____

City & State:_____Zip:_____

Credit Card #:_____Expires:_____

More Books By or About Dean Burgon
[ ] Send *Summary of Traditional Text* by Dr. Waite ($5 +$4)
[ ] Send *Summary of Causes of Corruption*, DAW ($5+$4)
[ ] Send *Summary of Inspiration* by Dr. Waite ($5+$4 S&H)

More Books by Dr. D. A. Waite
[ ] Send *Making Marriage Melodious* by Pastor D. A. Waite ($7+$5 S&H), perfect bound, 112 pages

Books by D. A. Waite, Jr.
[ ] Send *Readability of A.V. (KJB)* by D. A. Waite, Jr. ($7+$4)
[ ] Send *4,114 Definitions from the Defined King James Bible* by D. A. Waite, Jr. ($7.00+$5.00 S&H)
[ ] Send *The Doctored New Testament* by D. A. Waite, Jr. ($25+$7.00 S&H) Greek MSS differences shown, hardback
[ ] Send *Defined King James Bible* lg. prt. leather ($40+$10)
[ ] Send *Defined King James Bible* med. leather $35+$8.50)

Miscellaneous Authors
[ ] Send *The Attack on the Canon of Scripture* by Dr. H. D. Williams, perfect bound ($15.00 + $7.00 S&H)
[ ] Send *Word-For-Word Translating of The Received Texts* by Dr. H. D. Williams, 288 pages, paperback ($10+$7 S&H).
[ ] Send *Guide to Textual Criticism* by Edward Miller ($11+$7 S&H) a hardback book
[ ] Send *Scrivener's Greek New Testament Underlying the King James Bible*, hardback, ($14 + $7 S&H)
[ ] Send *Scrivener's Annotated Greek New Testament*, by Dr. Frederick Scrivener: Hardback--($35+$7 S&H); Genuine Leather--($45+$7 S&H)

Send or Call Orders to:
THE BIBLE FOR TODAY
900 Park Ave., Collingswood, NJ 08108
Phone: 856-854-4452; FAX:--2464; Orders: 1-800 JOHN 10:9
E-Mail Orders: BFT@BibleForToday.org; Credit Cards OK

Order Blank (p. 7)

Name:_____

Address:_____

City & State:_____Zip:_____

Credit Card #:_____Expires:_____

Miscellaneous Authors (Continued)

[ ] Send *Why Not the King James Bible?--An Answer to James White's KJVO Book* by Dr. K. D. DiVietro, $10+$7 S&H

[ ] Send Brochure #1: "Over *1000 Titles Defending the KJB/TR"* Compiled by Dr. D. A. Waite. No Charge

[ ] Send *Messages From the 2013 Dean Burgon Society* meeting. 197 pp. $18.00 + $7.00 S&H

Send or Call Orders to:
THE BIBLE FOR TODAY
900 Park Ave., Collingswood, NJ 08108
Phone: 856-854-4452; FAX:--2464; Orders: 1-800 JOHN 10:9
E-Mail Orders: BFT@BibleForToday.org; Credit Cards OK

The Defined King James Bible

Uncommon Words Defined Accurately

I. Deluxe Genuine Leather

✦Large Print--Black or Burgundy✦
1 for $40.00+$10.00 S&H
✦Case of 12 for $360.00✦
$30.00 each+$35 S&H

✦Medium Print--Black or Burgundy✦
1 for $35.00+$8.50 S&H
✦Case of 12 for $300.00✦
$25.00 each+$25 S&H

II. Deluxe Hardback Editions

1 for $20.00+$10.00 S&H (Large Print)
✦Case of 12 for $180.00✦
$15.00 each+$35 S&H (Large Print)
1 for $15.00+$7.50 S&H (Medium Print)
✦Case of 12 for $120.00✦
$10.00 each+$25 S&H (Medium Print)

Order Phone: 1-800-JOHN 10:9

Credit Cards Welcomed

Pastor D. A. Waite, Th.D., Ph.D.
Biblical Separation

- **The Reason For This Book.** We are living today when, after almost two thousand years since the New Testament was completed, many genuine born-again Christians seem to have no idea what *Biblical Separation* is all about. Because of this, this subject should be studied and explained clearly for everyone who wishes to read about it.
- **The Background of This Book.** The first draft of *Biblical Separation* was written in 1954 while the author was a graduate student at Dallas Theological Seminary in Texas. The book was revised in both 1971 and 1997. Finally, in 2014, the book has been published for all to look into.
- **The Method Used in This Book.** The author went through the Bible from Genesis through Revelation several times. He wanted to find out what the Bible teaches on the subject of *Bible Separation*. He noted every Bible verse in the Old and New Testaments that dealt with this theme whether directly or by illustration. There are 1,896 verses in all.
- **The Organization of This Book.** In these 130 pages, this important topic of *Biblical Separation* has been divided into six chapters: (1) Preliminary Considerations (2) Separation Regarding Things; (3) Separation Regarding Marriage; (4) Separation Regarding Unbelievers; (5) Separation Regarding Disorderly Believers; and (6) Summary And Conclusions. These chapters are followed by 9 pages of Scripture passages and index of subjects. May the Lord use this book for His glory to wake up genuinely saved Christians to follow God's standards regarding *Biblical Separation*.

www.BibleForToday.org

BFT #4087   ISBN #978-1-56848-992-6

CPSIA information can be obtained
at www.ICGtesting.com
Printed in the USA
LVHW012137090523
746583LV00028B/847

9 781568 489926